Flashes From The Past
Forty-Two Years Covering the News

Frank J. Kennedy

BREAKWATER

BREAKWATER
100 Water Street
P.O. Box 2188
St. John's, NF
A1C 6E6

Canadian Cataloguing in Publication Data
Kennedy, Frank J., 1921-
Flashes from the past: 42 years covering the news
ISBN 1-55081-164-9

I. Newfoundland--History--20th century--Miscellanea.
2. Newfoundland--History--20th century--Pictorial works.
3. History, Modern--20th century--Miscellanea.
4. History Modern--20th century--Pictorial works.
5. Kennedy, Frank J., 1921- I. Title

TR140.K39A3 2000   971.8'04   C00-901653-8

Copyright © 2000 - Frank J. Kennedy

The Canada Council | Le Conseil des Arts
for the Arts | du Canada

We acknowledge the financial support of The Canada Council for the Arts
for our publishing activities.

Canadä   We acknowledge the financial support of the Government of Canada through the Book Publishing Industry Development Program (BPIDP) for our publishing activities.

Printed in Canada.

DEDICATION

I dedicate this book to my wife Ruth, for her great encouragement and support.

To my daughter Florence, for persuading me at the outset to buy a computer.

To Glen Power for teaching me how to use it , and for transferring the 60,000 words to a disk for the publisher.

To my grandson Geoffrey, for the many times he solved unexpected problems that arose due to my inexperience with the computer.

I also want to express sincere thanks to Ms. Millie Hammond, Joan Grandy and Mr. David Leamen of the Reference Library for their kindness and efficiency in searching for old *Daily News* files, and Mr. Wayne Sturge of the Provincial Archives for his help in finding old photographs.

Special thanks to Mr. Clyde Rose and Ms. Carla Kean for undertaking the publishing of this book.

Thank you all.

CONTENTS

Flashes From The Past
Forty-Two Years Covering the News

Chapter One: The Early Years

Spies at Gander, 1941

I began my career as a professional photographer during the war years in Gander. On my very first assignment I was nearly arrested as a German spy. Indeed, there were German spies in Gander at the time, and two of them got away with a very important document. In 1941 I worked as a general office clerk in the Engineering Department of the Atlas Construction company. This company was building the base for the Royal Canadian Air Force (RCAF), consisting of twelve aircraft hangars and more than one hundred other buildings, all going up simultaneously. The company had more than two thousand men working there; this was long before the town of Gander came into existence. Part of the Engineering office's routine was to have progress photographs taken every two weeks or so. These photos were sent to the RCAF headquarters in Ottawa. This photography was part of a full time position, and the man who did it was our architect, Walt MacDonald. He had to have a special permit, as cameras were not allowed on base. Walt had given his notice, and our boss, Mr. Wilcox, asked me if I would like to take on the job along with my other duties, as he knew I was an amateur photographer. I was glad to accept the job.

On the very day Walt was to go, a request came in from headquarters for a picture of a particular building. Walt told the boss he had too much work to finish up, and asked if I could do the job. I interrupted, "But I don't have my permit yet!" MacDonald said he would lend me his. In those days (fifty-six years ago) before Polaroid cameras, it was not unusual for ID cards to have no photographs, just signatures. For added security we were also finger-printed. I took the permit and camera, jumped into a company car, and drove to the construction site. As I was taking the pictures, I heard the sound of a vehicle making an abrupt stop behind me. Looking around, I saw an RCAF officer rushing towards me, hand on side-arm holster. "What are you doing?" he shouted. I told him that I was taking a progress photo of the building for the RCAF, and showed him MacDonald's permit. Observing that I was not in uniform, he said he knew nothing about any progress photos, and that he thought he should get to a phone and check this out. I quickly explained that progress photography had been going on since construction of the base started, and that the Air Force had asked Atlas Construction to do it. "As a matter of fact ", I said, "your photo lab here on the base develops all the films for us. Then we identify the pictures, date them, and send them to your headquarters in Ottawa." I must have been convincing, for he handed the permit back to me and said, "All right, Mr. MacDonald, I guess it's all right." I went back to the office as fast as I could. I told the story to the boys and about how frightened I was; of course they all laughed. Soon after that, I received my own permit and had no further trouble, except for one time when an RCAF officer actually pulled a gun as he approached me. The base was literally crawling and I was often challenged. I really enjoyed the look of disbelief and caution on some of their faces as they came charging towards me with the demand "What the hell are you doing?" Of course when I produced the permit everything was okay.

Real Spies

In our engineering office we had what was called a "Plot Plan." This was a detailed drawing of the whole base, showing the location of all the hangers, the other buildings, and the aviation gasoline storage tanks which were about two miles from the runways. Part of my job was to make blueprints from this drawing, and make sure we always had copies on hand. The blueprints were about three feet square; although they were supposed to be secret, some of the foremen and engineers had copies. It required no special skill to make these blueprints with proper equipment; it was like making a photograph from a negative. While I did make a lot of copies, I was not authorized to give any out; nor did I. One day, however, two men dressed in RCAF uniforms walked into the office, showed some ID's and said they wanted a Plot Plan for the Base Commander. One of our staff checked their identification, which looked okay, gave them the blueprint, and got them to sign for it. Shortly after they left, it occurred to him that it was unusual for the Commander not to telephone and request the document. He called the Commander and gave the names of the two "officers" who had picked up the plan. The Commander had never heard of them! An extensive search was immediately held, but the two men were never found.

The location of the gasoline storage tanks would have been of immense value to the Germans, had they ever gotten around to dropping bombs on Newfoundland. It would have devastated the RAF Ferry Command Operation. This was a

Lockheed Hudson bomber on the grounds of the North Atlantic Museum at Gander. During World War Two, 6500 of these planes refueled at Gander en route from California to Great Britain. *Photo by Frank Kennedy*

tremendous undertaking during the war wherein Lockheed Hudson bombers manufactured in California for the United Kingdom, were flown to Gander for refueling before flying across the Atlantic. Sixty-five hundred Hudson bombers went through Gander during the war, and the United States Air Force (USAF) delivered no less than ten thousand aircraft to Europe from Gander Airport. (These figures are recorded in a 1992 Transport Canada publication, *History Of Canadian Airports* by T. M. McGrath.)

One can imagine the vast quantities of fuel that had to be kept on hand to supply such an enormous demand. The gasoline came into Gander from Lewisporte, thirty-two miles west of Gander, and was brought in by Shell tanker trucks. One bomb dropped in the right place would sabotage all this; and now the Germans knew this location!

Mysterious military plane crash near Gander during WW.II. Nothing was ever published. *Photo by Frank Kennedy*

After the war one of the Hudsons was flown back to Gander and now rests on the grounds of the North Atlantic Museum, on the Trans-Canada Highway near the entrance to the town of Gander. On many nights the sound of the bombers kept us awake as they roared over our bunkhouse on their way across the ocean. We were glad they were not dropping anything on us!

Generally speaking, security was very good at Gander during the war. For instance, a large military aircraft crashed about one mile north of the base with reported loss of life, and not one word got to the media. Nothing! Some weeks later, two co-workers and myself found our way to the crash site. I had my small folding camera tucked away out of sight, and got a couple of pictures. I kept this roll of film and developed it myself when I got back to St. John's. These pictures have never been published until now.

The Knights of Columbus Fire

After a year at Gander, I came back to St. John's. I took a position as customs clerk with the wholesale dry goods firm of Garneau Limited, and so for two years reverted to the status of amateur photographer. (A professional photographer is a person who earns a living mainly from photographic work; it has nothing to do with the photographer's ability.) It was during this time that the Knights of Columbus fire took place, a disaster that took the lives of ninety-nine people. Although not working for the media at the time, I did take some pictures of the incident. I remember the night very well; it was December 12, 1942.

I worked in the office of Garneau Limited on Water Street, just east of Adelaide Street, with four young ladies. Two of these, Josephine Casey and Ida Allen, lived west as did I. On Saturday nights we worked until 9:30 p. m., and as the "blackout" was on, I would walk home with them. On this particular night they left work early and went just up the street to the Mount Cashel Raffle, to try their pre-Christmas luck for half-an-hour. Before leaving our office, they asked me to pick them up on my way home, which I did. As soon as I walked in the door of the Raffle, the "last six tickets" were pushed into my face by one of the vendors, so of course I bought them. Much to the disgust of the two lovely ladies, who were still empty-handed and almost empty-pursed, I won a nice pair of chickens! I laughed all the way home.

Later that night, we were sitting around at home when we heard a fire truck passing our front door on Patrick Street. We couldn't see out the window because of the blackout shutters, so I went outdoors and saw the fire truck going towards LeMarchant Road. Looking further east, I saw a bright orange glow in the sky. I went back into the house, got my folding camera, and ran up Patrick Street and across LeMarchant Road. By the time I reached the fire, most of the building was destroyed. I only had two snaps left on the roll of film, so I went first to the rear of the building and

Ninety-nine people died in the K. of C. Hostel fire in St. John's on Dec. 12, 1942. Members of Uncle Tim's Barn Dance troupe and some others escaped through the window shown here, which led from the stage in the auditorium *Photo by Frank Kennedy*

took a shot of the burning auditorium. The stage was at this end of the building, and some of the survivors escaped through the window shown in the picture.

A strange thing about this fire was that after it was first discovered, no one tried to send in an alarm to the fire department, except perhaps the Knights of Columbus' bookkeeper, John St. John. His body was found after the fire, at his desk with his charred hand still clutching the telephone receiver. He never got through. When first told about the fire, he ran upstairs to have a look, then ran back down into his office. That was the last time he was seen alive. Nearly twenty minutes later, Police Constable S. Reynolds, in a traffic control box a half-mile away on Rawlin's Cross, reported by telephone that he could see the flames of a large fire in the upper area of town. The fire hall was just down the road from the Knights of Columbus, and the firemen were on the scene in less than two minutes. By that time, nearly a hundred people were already dead or dying.

The Knights of Columbus Hostel was a two-storey wooden building erected a year earlier on Harvey Road, for the accommodation and entertainment of the Allied troops. Every Saturday night, a musical group under the direction of Joe Murphy staged a concert in the auditorium, which was broadcast live on the radio station VOCM. It was billed as "Uncle Tim's Barn Dance" and was very popular. On the fatal night, nearly four hundred soldiers, sailors, women and children were seated and enjoying the show. Upstairs, a soldier walked down a hallway form a dormitory looking for a washroom. Thinking he'd found one, he opened the door and to his horror was confronted by an inferno. It was a storage room all ablaze! Leaving the door open, he rushed down the hallway and down the stairs to sound the alarm. A Canadian sailor in the dorm saw him running and came out to investigate. He managed to force the door closed, but suffered severe burns in doing so. The storage room was located just over the projection room at the rear of the auditorium, and by now the fire had eaten down into that area. A commotion broke out in the rear of the auditorium; emcee Joe Murphy, thinking a fight had started, grabbed a microphone and urged the crowd to remain calm. Just then a woman screamed "Fire! Fire!"

The fuse panel for the lights in the auditorium was in the projection room; the heat of the fire melted the fuses and all the lights went out. There were no emergency lights, and the exit lights also failed. Flames shot along the ceiling of the auditorium and ignited the paper Christmas decorations which fell on the panic-stricken crowd, setting some of them on fire. The seats, which were folding metal chairs, were not fastened to the floor, and this added to the confusion as people fell over them in the dark. Those at the back of the auditorium rushed out through the rear doors, which opened into a restaurant, then through this room into the front lobby, and out the front door to safety. The whole U-shaped building had a sealed loft or attic with no vents, and as the fire burned along inside this large area, tremendous pressures of gas built up and started bursting downwards through the ceilings. When the door of the storage room burned through, the fire went rapidly through the hallway and down the

Last remaining section of front wall collapses during the inferno. *Photo by Frank Kennedy*

stairs with explosive force. Several of the people heading out through the lobby were actually blown out through the front door, suffering burns on the way.

This blast of superheated gas and flames now blocked those coming from the auditorium; they had to go back in and find another way out. There were three other exits, but they all had double doors. The inner doors opened inwards, and the outer doors were locked. With the crowd surging towards these, it was almost impossible to get them open. Finally, some servicemen linked hands and formed human chains to keep the people back and get the inner doors open. They then had to break through the outer doors. The carbon monoxide and other gases billowing down through the burning ceiling overcame many people before they could reach the exits. All the windows were fitted with plywood shutters, and in the darkness it was difficult to find the windows, let alone break them open.

The fire had now reached the stage, and Joe Murphy suggested that his crew should go into a small dressing room on the stage where there was a window just above ground level. Four of the members decided to go down into the main auditorium. Two of them helped the sailors and soldiers forming the human chains at the exits. They died in the attempt. The third, a Canadian sailor, jumped off the stage in an effort to rescue his girlfriend who was in the audience. He must have fallen, for he was later found crushed to death. His girlfriend was saved by two other sailors who found her in a dazed condition and threw her out a window. The fourth was the sixteen-year-old drummer, Derm Duggan. He was nearly overcome by the smoke, and a large American soldier tripped over him as he lay on the floor. The soldier picked him up and got him out through one of the side doors. That brave man was last seen going back into the burning auditorium. Young Duggan spent several weeks in hospital recovering from severe burns.

On the stage, some members of the band smashed the shutter on the window in the dressing room. Joe Murphy helped get the rest of his crew out, as well as some others who had come up from the auditorium, before jumping himself. His own clothing caught fire just before he escaped; he was the last person to go through that window. In the front section of the building a reading room opened off the restaurant and several people sought refuge there. They were helped out through windows by people outside who had escaped the burning building earlier. Ninety-nine people died, and more than one hundred people were injured in the blaze. All ambulances in the city were called to the scene and a city bus waited nearby to bring many of the walking injured to St. Clare's Hospital for treatment. An extensive inquiry involving 178 witnesses concluded that the fire was deliberately set, but whether it was the work of an enemy agent or a pyromaniac still remains a mystery.

The Gander Crash

Many U.S. servicemen died in the tragic Knights of Columbus fire. It is a sad coincidence that on the same date, December 12, 1986, forty-four years later, two hundred and forty-eight U.S. servicemen were killed in the Arrow plane crash at Gander. In that tragedy the soldiers, part of a U.N. Peacekeeping Force serving in the Middle East, were returning on Christmas leave to their home base in Fort Campbell, Kentucky. They were members of the 101st Airborne Division, and were on the last leg of a journey that originated in Cairo, Egypt, with refueling stops at Cologne, West Germany and Gander, Newfoundland. The plane, a chartered Arrow Air DC 8, barely lifted off the runway, passed over the Trans-Canada Highway and crashed down in the woods just short of Gander Lake killing all on board including the eight crew members. Icing of the wings was thought to be the probable cause of the accident. CBC cameraman Larry Hudson scooped the world with his exclusive shots of the crash site. Larry was on the scene so quickly after the plane came down, that the wreckage was still burning and police lines had not yet been put in place. No other media member got anywhere near the site, as the RCAF soon took charge and secured the area, along with the RCMP. Larry was horrified at the sight of so many bodies strewn about, and to his everlasting credit he filmed none of these, bearing in mind that this film would probably be seen in the United States and he hated the thought of some mother recognizing her son's body. He was right about the film being seen in the U. S. In fact it was used over and over world-wide, this being the only film of the worst plane crash ever on Canadian soil.

A beautiful monument now stands at the site on the shore of Gander Lake. It is a larger-than-life bronze statue of an Airborne Division soldier, holding the hands of a little girl and boy and facing the direction in which the aircraft was heading: Kentucky, U.S.A. The very touching work, titled "The Silent Witness," was designed by well-known professional photographer, Lorne Rostotski of St. John's, and was crafted by Stephen Shields of Kentucky, home state of the 101st Division.

"The Silent Witness." Beautiful larger-than-life monument stands at the crash site in Gander, as a memorial to the two hundred and forty-eight U.S. servicemen who died in the Arrow Air plane crash on December 12, 1986. *Photo by Frank Kennedy*

Chapter Two: The *Daily News* Years

M. S. Clarenville: Truly Launched, Not Properly Christened

I started as press photographer with the St. John's *Daily News* in late March, 1944. After two weeks I was given my first out-of-town assignment: to cover the launching of the first ship of the so called "Splinter Fleet," a series of five wooden ships being built at Clarenville. This was a really big deal. The Commission of Government even provided a special train to take the VIPs and press to Clarenville from St. John's. The train had dining and sleeping cars; we had sumptuous meals and sleeping accommodations. On the train were: Lieutenant Governor Walwyn and Lady Walwyn; most of the members of the Commission of Government; the Superintendent of Newfoundland Dockyards, Mr. R. Thompson; President of the Board of Trade, Mr. J. B. Angel; and many other dignitaries. The train arrived in Clarenville just

The *M.V. Clarenville* slides into North West Arm at launching. Note unbroken bottle of champagne dangling from the bow which the boys smartly pulled up and drank! (arrow) Daily News *Photo by Frank Kennedy*

before midnight and the nearly forty people spent the night on board. After breakfast next morning, we proceeded to the ship-yard for the ceremony. It was April 12, 1944. Thousands of spectators were on hand to see the big event.

The *Daily News* on the following day proclaimed with big headlines: "Clarenville Slides Down Ways Amid Great Rejoicing," and in smaller print, "As workmen knocked away the props, Lady Walwyn pronounced the traditional formula, 'I name this ship Clarenville; may God bless all who sail in her,' and swung the time-honored bottle of champagne upon the bow." The bottle hit the bow all right, but it didn't break and Lady Walwyn had no second chance, as the ship was already sliding down the slipway out of reach, with the bottle dangling on a rope from the deck. There was even more rejoicing as the men on board took advantage of this unexpected development, hoisted the champagne on board and happily drank it. No proper christening here! That "misfire" was never before reported, but that is how it happened.

Later that same year, we covered the big fire in Harbour Grace that destroyed the whole waterfront section of town. Forty-two business establishments and dozens of houses were burned to the ground, leaving one 125 families homeless.

The Harbour Grace Conflagration of 1944

We heard about the fire early in the afternoon of August 18th. Honorable J. S. Currie, our publisher, instructed his chauffeur, Hayward Pike, to drive reporter Doug Payne and myself to the town in his big blue Nash. There was no Trans-Canada Highway in those days and it took two hours to drive the sixty-four miles around the bay on mostly unpaved roads. When we finally arrived at the west end of town we met a scene of total devastation. Smoking ruins all around! We got out of the car and told our driver to go down to Archibald's Hotel, more than a mile along the road at the other end of Harbour Grace, and order a meal. We would be along in an hour or so after we'd taken some pictures.

Good photography was difficult, as there was thick smoke everywhere. Having taken several shots and being rather hungry by now, not to mention thirsty, Payne and I walked through the smoke to the location of Archibald's Hotel. Our driver was there alright, but the hotel was gone— burned to the ground. No supper that day! The fire started in Parson's Jam Factory on Water Street, in their small warehouse behind the main plant. The exact cause was never determined, as no one was in that building at the time and the fire was well under way by the time it was discovered. The fire hall was nearby, but when the volunteer fire brigade got to the scene, the building was a mass of flames. A strong westerly wind was blowing and the fire soon began to spread. The fire hall caught fire, and when the tower supporting the large fire-bell burned through, the bell that in the past had alerted residents of a fire in town, went crashing to the ground with an ominous and final loud clang. When the fire reached Babbs' premises, further along Water Street, a number of casks of gasoline stored there exploded and accelerated the blaze. The

Chimneys line the waterfront in Harbour Grace after devastating fire on August 18, 1944. *Photo by Frank Kennedy*

three lines of hose in use by the volunteer firemen were totally inadequate, and the fire was now completely out of control, so calls went out for assistance.

Very soon, no less than seven fire trucks were racing to the scene from Carbonear, Whitbourne and St. John's, including two from the Royal Canadian Navy in the capital city. By the time help arrived from St. John's, however, both sides of Water Street for more than a mile were on fire; efforts could only be made to save the rest of the town. Flankers had blown along in the wind, landed on roofs and caused many separate outbreaks. The United Church and parsonage were destroyed in this way. St. Paul's Anglican Church also caught fire, but it was put out by parishioners guarding it. At Simmons Brothers, five hundred tons of coal caught fire and was burning for days. S.W. Moores had just built a large fish plant at the cost of nearly half a million dollars and employing over one hundred people. Although it was a concrete building, it too was completely destroyed along with Moores' General Store. It had only been open for a week. Men

Firemen hose down hot spots on Water Street, against a background of burned out Post Office. Daily News *Photo by Frank Kennedy*

working on the fish wharf behind the plant were cut off by the flames and had to be rescued by boat.

The stone and concrete two-storey post office building was wiped out; however, all the mail had been removed when it was seen that the building was doomed. Other buildings to go were two hotels, two restaurants, the police station, customs office, several shops and the telephone exchange building. Amazingly, with such widespread destruction, there were no serious injuries, although in some cases the fire spread so rapidly that people fled their homes without saving any belongings. In one case, Head Constable Bussy entered a burning home and rescued a three-year-old child from an upstairs bedroom. His uniform caught fire as he rushed out the front door but a fireman quickly quenched the blaze, and neither he nor the child was injured.

Many people removed furniture from their homes and placed it on the sidewalks and streets but none of it escaped the flames. A truck loaded with furniture even caught fire as it was moving away, but that fire was put out with little damage. The fire was declared under control by 6 p. m., but the St. John's firemen stayed all night putting out hot spots and flare-ups. The next day, three truckloads of food—enough for at least six hundred meals—were sent over by the Royal Canadian Navy in St. John's; also, six carloads of provisions went by train and a Red Cross truck brought in three thousand pieces of clothing. Estimated damage at the time was four million dollars; a lot of money fifty years ago!

Other Local News Items for the Year 1944

Jan. 17	Hawthorne Cottage, a boarding house on Carter's Hill, badly damaged by fire. Three families left homeless.
Jan. 21	Mr. Eric Bowring presents yacht, *Happy Adventure* to the Lord Bishop of Newfoundland, to be used in his work around the shores of the island.

Jan. 31	Cave-in at Fluorspar Mines in St. Lawrence. One man injured.
Feb. 1	Roman Catholic Deanery on Patrick Street in St. John's badly damaged by fire.
Apr. 4	*S. S. Eagle*, the only ship to take part in this year's seal fishery, finishes discharging in St. John's. Total catch 6697 seals. The crew shared $48.31 per man.
May 11	Second "Splinter Fleet" vessel launched at Clarenville. Christened Burin by Mrs. J. A. Burden.
May 13	First all-steel train in Newfoundland given trial run. It will be called *The Overland Limited*; it was later known as *The Newfie Bullet*.
Aug. 16	Train derailment near Bonavista sends locomotive and tender over 80 foot embankment. Four men injured.
Aug. 28	S. S. Kyle runs aground at Englee, North of White Bay, on the Great Northern Peninsula. Later refloated but damaged.
Sept. 1	New Paramount Movie Theater on Harvey Road officially opened.
Sept. 5	*S. S. Kyle* arrives in St. John's to have grounding damage repaired.
Oct. 24	St. John's Deputy Mayor Cook turns first sod of new village in North East St. John's. New road will be called Elizabeth Avenue.
Oct. 30	Bell Island mines cut to three day work week.

The Liquor Control Building Fire and the Day the *Daily News* Went Blank

Early Sunday morning on April 22, 1945, a fire erupted on Duckworth Street in St. John's. It destroyed the six-storey United Towns building and the three-storey Liquor Control building. When the next issue of the *Daily News* hit the streets from the publishing building, two doors west of the fire, page one looked good, but pages two, three and four were completely blank. There was an amusing connection!

The fire was first reported at 2:14 a.m. by an Avalon Telephone operator, working across the street from the United Towns building where the fire started. At the same time, an alarm came in from a box at the foot of McBride's Hill on Water Street. When fireman arrived minutes later from the Central Fire Station, they found flames coming from the top three floors of the United Towns building. Immediately, Fire Chief Blackburn called for help from the East and West End stations. Several lines of hose were quickly laid out, and firemen fought the blaze from McBride's Hill, from Duckworth Street, and from the roof of the adjoining Liquor Control building. In minutes however, the fire spread to that building, and the firemen had to retreat to the roof of the building next door, Clancy & Company, and continue the battle from there. Separating Clancy & Company from the *Daily News* building was a ten-foot driveway. Both roofs were on almost the same level, so the firemen put a ladder across, forming a bridge between the two structures.

As the fire grew worse, an explosion blew out part of the rear wall of the Liquor building and the flaming roof began to collapse. Once more the firemen had to retreat, and ran across the ladder to the *Daily News* building. Fortunately, a thick brick wall separated the Liquor Board and Clancy buildings and the fire could not penetrate this barrier. Firemen working with two hoses from the roof of the news building prevented Clancy's roof from igniting. In the meantime, with the roofs of the two burning buildings now gone, and flames reaching thirty feet in the air, sparks and flankers began falling on the block of houses on City

Terrace across the street. Chief Blackburn ordered his men to get a hose up to the roof of this block, and so the fire was prevented from spreading in that direction. By now, the Royal Canadian Navy had sent nearly a hundred men under the direction of Fire Marshall Warren, R. C. N., with pumps and searchlights to help city firemen. The local Auxiliary Fire Services were also called in.

When the rear wall blew out, most of the debris fell on the roof of Pope's Furniture Factory on Water Street. Blackburn feared the fire might spread to the Water Street buildings. Luckily, the Navy men pumped water from the St. John's Harbour, and prevented this from happening. When the fire spread west to the Liquor Board building, it was thought it might reach the *Daily News* office, so management there called in some of the printers to perhaps remove some valuable equipment, should destruction of that building become inevitable. These *Daily News* men went on their roof and helped with the hoses. Two hours after the fire started, fourteen streams of water were being played on the burning buildings, as well as one across the street on City Terrace. Fire Chief Blackburn said later," I wouldn't say we had the fire under complete control until 5:30 a.m. When Clancy's was threatened, I reorganized the fire defenses in front, and had ladders raised to the windows of the Board of Liquor Control. The men, under difficult circumstances, yet working diligently and heroically, fought the flames back to the United Towns building."

The Connection

When dawn came at about six o'clock, the fire was dying down and the firemen removed their hoses from the *Daily News* building. The "news" men went back on the roof of Clancy & Company and looked down into the now wide-open top floor of the Liquor Board building. What they saw were firemen, now inside, putting out some hot spots, amidst thousands of bottles of liquor, rum, whiskey and gin scattered around in the wet charred surroundings. The firemen saw the men who had been helping them earlier, and began tossing up bottles of liquor. Most of the labels had been soaked off in the water from the fire hoses. In true baseball style, not a bottle was dropped, and all the catches were perfect. The printers took their loot down through a hatch in the roof of the news building, and on down to the pressroom without the knowledge of management. The bottles were stashed away under the huge rolls of newsprint, and this being a

United Towns, Liquor Store, Clancy's and Daily News buildings as they stand today. Dotted line indicates original height of Liquor Building at time of fire on April 22, 1945. Four stories were later added. *Photo by Frank Kennedy*

Sunday morning, there was no paper published, so the printers went home. Monday was a holiday, being St. George's Day, so there was no paper that day either. But on Monday night when the pressroom staff came in at eleven o'clock to get Tuesday's edition ready, they got into the cache of goodies, and had a ball. By the time Tuesday's issue rolled of the press, the "boys" were feeling great, and while page one looked good, (all ads in those days), pages two, three and four were completely blank! The levels of blood-alcohol certainly had a deteriorating effect on the printers' workmanship. Hundreds of copies were sent around to shops, etc. , before the blunder was discovered. When the day shift came in at 8 a. m., the press was re-plated and a proper run was made. Management were not amused, especially the publisher, the late Honorable J. S. Currie, a very respectable statesman, and a nondrinker. If blame could have been placed on the shoulders of just one or two employees, they could have been discharged, but Mr. Currie was not about to fire the whole pressroom. Also, it was not something that was likely to happen again. To his credit, the gentleman let the matter drop; but it was a day long remembered at the *Daily News*.

German Submarine Surrenders

Three days after World War Two ended, a German U-Boat surfaced 450 miles off the coast of Newfoundland and surrendered to two Canadian warships. The sub was to be escorted into Bay Bulls, and *Daily News* reporters Doug Payne and I were assigned to the story. We drove the eighteen miles to Bay Bulls and arrived just at dawn. The sub had not yet arrived, so, thinking we might go out and get some pictures of the convoy on its way in, we looked around for a boat that we could hire. We saw only one fishing boat that seemed ready to go and we asked the owner if he could take us out. The man asked if we were from *The Evening Telegram*, the evening paper that had hired him, and naturally Doug Payne said we were. So out we went.

We sighted the sub a few miles outside Bay Bulls harbour, with a warship (corvette) on each side and followed by several Q-boats and a tug. Payne thought it would be nice if we could get between one of the corvettes and the sub, to get some close-ups. We were just in position when a loudspeaker on the warship announced that if we didn't get out of there at once, they would blow us out of the water! Perhaps they were joking, but our boat owner took no chances and took off.

A few days earlier, the submarine had signaled its position to the Royal Canadian Naval authorities in St. John's and the two Canadian corvettes, *H. M. C. S. Victoriaville* and *H. M. C. S. Thorlock*, which were escorting a convoy across the Atlantic, broke away from that duty and went to the reported location to make a search. It was Thursday, May 10, 1945. Shortly after 8:00 p. m. , Stoker Emilieu Houde of Ansonville, came on the bridge of the *Thorlock*, looked around and saw a dim glow. He alerted a signal man and pointed. Another officer grabbed a set of binoculars." It's the sub! "he shouted. It was 8:10 p. m. The ocean was calm and the U-boat was on the surface. As the corvette approached, they asked the craft to identify itself. They got no reply that they could decipher, but the German black flag of surrender was flying from the masthead. Very cautiously, the *Thorlock* came alongside. There was no one in sight. Lieutenant Ossie Blackford of Montreal jumped on the deck of the sub, followed by a ten-man boarding party. The conning tower hatch was open and Chief E. R. A. Stanley Deom was the first to go down into the sub. He confront-ed the Germans, who at first stared grimly at him. He was appre-hensive, as it occurred to him that he had no gun; he was very relieved when the sailors saluted him and began passing over their small weapons. Most of the members of the German crew were transferred to the *Victoriaville*, but two engineers remained to help the Canadian Navy men take the sub in to port. The sub-marine had been at sea forty-five days and looked as if it could really use a paint job. It was covered with barnacles and rust, indi-cating long service underwater. It was equipped with the Schnorkel breathing apparatus which can take in fresh air and discharge foul air and fumes while the sub is under water.

The crew of about thirty men were all quite young, in their twenties and thirties; even the captain seemed in his mid-twen-ties. All had beards at the time of surrender but most shaved them off during the three days it took to sail to Newfoundland. The Canadian Navy boys were amused that all the Germans, even the captain, got seasick on the way along. It seems they were not used to sailing on the surface of the ocean and the seas were rough. When the flotilla reached Bay Bulls on May 15th, the German crew were brought ashore under heavy guard and trans-ferred to another ship to go to Halifax. The captain was still below deck, and reporter Payne tried to get an interview with him. He was told by the Canadian Naval Intelligence officer, that under the terms of the Geneva Convention, no interview was possible

German submarine U-190 enters St. John's Harbour in 1945. Now crewed by Canadian Navy members, it had spent three weeks at Bay Bulls after surrender. Daily News *Photo by Frank Kennedy. Courtesy Doug Payne.*

without the consent of the captain, and he refused, so that ended that. Nevertheless, Payne tried to sneak below deck, but was stopped and unceremoniously escorted ashore.

I asked for a group photo of the German crew before they were put aboard the internment ship, and this was thought by the Navy to be okay. When the men lined up in front of me, one of them said something in German, which sounded like, "Les-hel-en" and was probably, "Smile!" for they all did smile as my flash bulb went off. At least six of them wore the Iron Cross, signifying outstanding bravery in action. They all seemed happy as they went aboard the other ship. Then the young German captain appeared on the deck of the *Victoriaville*. He was now smiling and stopped to shake hands with some of the Canadian officers, including the captain, Lieutenant Commander Hickey, who happened to be a Newfoundlander from St. Jacques, Fortune Bay. He thanked the men for what they had done and stepped onto the gangplank to leave the ship. Then he saw our camera and stopped smiling. He put his hand up to shield his face as the camera flashed, and said in English, "It's not fair!"

CANADA

Department of National Defence

Naval Service

IN REPLY PLEASE QUOTE

NO.

12. ..... 02 ᵒᵘ 9.9.3. ..... 1945.

I hereby unconditionally surrender German
Submarine U 190 to the Royal Canadian Navy
through the Flag Officer Newfoundland.

~Commanding Officer~

Surrender document was typed on Canadian naval stationary and signed by the U-Boat Commander. *Courtesy Doug Payne*

While on board the *Victoriaville*, he had signed the surrender document in the presence of the Newfoundland captain. It was written on a National Defense Naval Service letterhead and read: "I hereby unconditionally surrender German Submarine U-190 to the Royal Canadian Navy through Flag Officer Newfoundland " (Signed by the Commanding Officer, U-190). Later that afternoon the Lieutenant Governor, Sir Humphrey Walwyn, visited the submarine, accompanied by other dignitaries including Sir Albert Walsh and Col. L. C. Outerbridge. The U-Boat remained in Bay Bulls for three weeks, and was a big tourist attraction, as thousands of people came to see the war prize. Then it went on to St. John's, where again it was seen by thousands of interested people, before going to the Navy Yard in Halifax.

Indeed, it was a valuable war prize, for this multi-million dollar submarine was only three years old, and was equipped with the most modern equipment. In June, 1945, it was commissioned into the Canadian Navy and re-named the *H. M. C. S. U-190* and served as a training ship for more than two years.

Originally, when the U-190 surrendered, it was to be escorted to the Naval Headquarters in Halifax. But just three weeks before the war ended, this same sub had sunk a Canadian Navy Mine sweeper, the *H. M. C. S. Esquimalt*, just outside Halifax Harbour with a loss of forty-four lives (twenty-seven men survived). It was therefore felt by the authorities that to bring that sub back to Halifax could well result in a violent confrontation with the inhabitants, so the decision was taken to bring the U-boat to Newfoundland.

In October, 1947, the *H. M. C. S. U-190* was towed to the very spot where the minesweeper *Esquimalt* went down, and in a classic Naval exercise, was blasted with heavy Canadian Navy gunfire and sank beneath the waves, to rest on the bottom of the Atlantic side by side with its former victim. Before the final sinking near Halifax, the sub's periscope was removed, and in 1963 was presented to the Officers' Club (The Crow's Nest) in St. John's, where to this day it is still in use, offering a fine view of the narrows and St. John's Harbour.

Other Local News Events for the Year 1945

Jan. 9	Asst. Chief of Police Strange appointed to succeed the late Patrick J. O'Neill as chief of Police.
Jan. 25	New General Hospital on Quidi Vidi Road opened to visitors.
Feb. 2	New Boys' Home and Training School opened at Whitbourne.
Feb. 18	Fire damages roof of Wesley United Church on Patrick Street.
Feb. 19	Formal opening new convent in St. Teresa's Parish, Mundy Pond.
Feb. 20	Jessie Froud, twenty-one, resident of Somerset, T. B., charged with the murder of her child.

Mar. I	Estimated damage by fire at Port Union over one million dollars.
Mar. 25	Fire at Gray & Goodland premises on Water Street causes $15,000 damage.
May 11	St. John's blacked out as child throws wire over transformer at main substation nearLong Bridge.
May 15	Railway ship Moyra and cargo total loss.
June 11	Thirty-five year-old Rolls-Royce car imported by Sir Edgar Bowring in 1910, makes reappearance on St. John's streets.
June 16	Gerald Hollett, eighteen year-old troop leader of Burin Boy Scouts, awarded Gilt Cross for gallantry during fire at Burin school.
June 21	New St. Kevin's Church in Goulds formally opened.
June 24	Consecration ceremony at Roman Catholic Cathedral of Most Reverend Thomas J. Flynn, D.D., as Coadjutor Archbishop of St. John's. (He was to succeed Archbishop Roach, but died before him.)
June 29	Schooner *Gladys Mosher* wrecked at Cape Ray. No lives lost.
July 2	Eclipse of the Sun visible in Newfoundland.
July 3	Basil Young, seventeen, of Lourdes, Port au Port, charged with the murder of his father, William V. Young, forty-seven.
July 5	Canadian Army helps rebuild Harbour Grace. Donated barracks material, lumber and supplies.

July 19	Forest fire destroys several buildings in St. Mary's Harbour, Southern Labrador.
July 28	Large draft of Royal Navy men arrive home from the war.
July 30	First batch 59th Heavy Regiment arrives home for demobilization.
Aug. 3	Ocean liner *Drottingholm* arrives St. John's with wives and families of Newfoundland servicemen who married while overseas. Second draft of Royal Artillery arrives home.
Aug. 14 & 15	V. J. Day Celebrated. (Victory in Japan).
Aug. 17	Farewell luncheon for Honorable P. D .H. Dunn, OB.E., Commissioner of Natural Resources, who is returning to England.
Aug. 22	General Charles de Gaulle visits Gander, en route to United States.
Aug. 23	Third draft Royal Artillery arrives home.
Aug. 25	Newfoundland Light & Power Company announces reduction in electricity rates.
Sep. 3	U. S. troops leave Newfoundland for home.
Sep. 8	Well known one hundred-year-old Topsail resort, "Berg's ", destroyed by fire.
Sep. 14	*M. V. Gertrude* destroyed by fire at Belleoram.
Oct. 24	Murder trial seventeen year-old Basil Young concluded. He was found guilty and sentenced to life in prison.
Nov. 18	Boy's Home at Whitbourne destroyed by fire.

Captain Bob Bartlett Buried In Home Town

The body of world-famous Arctic explorer, Captain Bob Bartlett, was laid to rest in the family plot on a hill overlooking his home town of Brigus on May 8, 1946. Born in 1875, Bartlett was best known as the captain of the ship that took Robert Peary on the expedition that would result in the controversial discovery of the North Pole in 1909. Peary had been trying for ten years to reach this goal, and with Bartlett, had made three serious attempts. Peary was the world-renowned American Arctic explorer who, among other accomplishments, proved in 1892 that Greenland was an island. Various European explorers had been trying to reach the Pole by crossing over Greenland, but Peary decided on a more westerly route.

The first expedition set out in 1898 from New York. Bartlett, who was only twenty-three at the time, signed on as first mate on Peary's ship, the *Windward*. This was at the invitation of the ship's master, Captain John Bartlett, his uncle, who was also a Newfoundlander (as were most of the crew). Heading north to Etah, an Inuit settlement on the north-west coast of Greenland 200 miles north of Thule, the Windward picked up several dog teams, many sleds and several dozen extra crew members, along with supplies from another of Peary's ships, the *Hope*, which had preceded the *Windward* from New York. From there, Peary and Bartlett hoped to get to the north coast of Ellesmere Island at the very top of the Northwest Territories, but the ship became frozen solid in the ice 300 miles from that goal. Knowing they would have to spend the winter there, the two explorers worked all winter with dog teams and sleds, driven by the Inuit, bringing supplies further north with the intention of trying for the Pole the following summer. It is interesting to note that, unlike the South Pole, there is no land at all at the North Pole; just water covered by a thick layer of ice, and the ocean is two miles deep!

By the time the ship was frozen in, there was perpetual darkness, and the traveling had to be done by the light of the moon. The extreme cold took its toll on Peary, and in the minus 45 degree temperature, his feet froze and gangrene set in. He spent two months in a small shack, 200 miles from his ship, while Bartlett and his men continued to bring supplies north. When daylight returned in the spring, Peary was strapped to a sled and brought back to the ship, where the ship's doctor amputated all his toes. Even this did not deter him from his aim, and he pushed forward with Bartlett's help, riding mostly on a sled pulled by a dog team. Finally, supplies and food began running short, and with many of the dogs dead, the expedition had to be abandoned. One thing Peary did learn from this experience was that if he were ever to try again for the Pole, Bob Bartlett would be indispensable. Try again he did, and Bartlett promised to go with him, for Bartlett loved the Arctic as much as Peary.

Peary spent years preparing for his second voyage, and even had a new ship built especially for Arctic travel, with the backing of some American millionaires. In the meantime, Captain Bartlett went to the ice (sealing) in the springs of 1903, 1904 and 1905. He was following in the footsteps of his father, grandfather, and great grandfather, who were all well known Newfoundland sealing captains.

In July 1905, the new ship *Roosevelt* sailed from New York with two years supplies on board. She stopped at Sydney, Nova Scotia, where Captain Bob Bartlett took command at the request of Peary. This time all the crew were Newfoundlanders, former sealers picked by Bartlett himself. Troubles began early on this trip, for shortly after leaving Nova Scotia two of the *Roosevelt's* three boilers blew up, cutting down the ship's speed considerably. Nevertheless, they decided to continue on, as the ship had sails as well as steam power. Stopping at Greenland once more, and picking up more supplies and Inuit crew they managed to reach Ellesmere Island by early September, as planned, and spend the winter there. Bartlett was now more than 2000 miles north of Brigus, a long way from home. Many of the crew went hunting, and thus stored up a good supply of meat for the coming months.

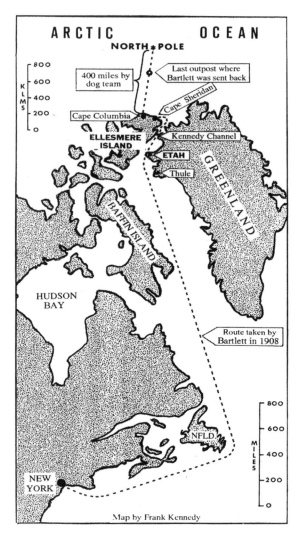

Map shows route taken by Bartlett and Peary on their controversial trip to the North Pole in 1909.

Starting out in mid-February 1906, Bartlett and his men began marking a route to the Pole for Peary, and set out with dog teams to place supplies at various points along the way, in igloos which they built for that purpose. This was so that Peary could travel lightly on the final leg of the journey. After three months of this strenuous work in bitterly cold weather, many of the dogs had died and supplies were running short, much of the food having been left in the snow houses further north. Another unforeseen problem was the existence of very long "leads "of open water which were impossible to cross with the sleds. Once more the courageous explorers had to give up and head for home. It was now early June 1906.

Their troubles were far from over, for soon after leaving Ellesmere Island, and heading for Greenland to drop off the Inuit crew, the ship struck an uncharted rock and badly damaged the rudder and the two propellers. The ship managed to limp into Etah, where repairs were made. Still more trouble occurred; after leaving Etah and spending nearly a week dropping off the Inuit to their various villages on the coast of Greenland, a severe storm hit the ship on the way to the Labrador coast, and this time the rudder was completely lost. They managed to rig some sort of steering apparatus, but then they ran out of coal. Burning whatever they could find on board, including some of the ship's furniture, they kept up enough steam to reach the coast, and stopping at several places in Labrador, were able to get enough spruce logs to steam south to Battle Harbour, a few miles north of the Strait of Belle Isle. In Battle Harbour they bought a supply of coal, but when the *Roosevelt* finally arrived in New York, on Christmas Eve, 1906, the return trip had taken more than three months.

In spite of all the hardships they had endured, Peary was determined to try again in two years if funding was available, and Bartlett again agreed to go with him, with the understanding that they would both go to the Pole. In the spring of 1907, Bartlett left St. John's in command of the sealing steamer *Leopard*, heading for the Gulf of St. Lawrence where seals were in abundance. There was heavy ice all along the east coast of the Avalon Peninsula, but open water close to shore. Bartlett decided to use this open water route, but 50 miles south of St. John's a strong easterly wind moved the ice in, and the *Leopard* was driven ashore near Cappahayden. The ship was a total loss, but Bartlett and all the crew got safely ashore.

In 1908 Bartlett once more took command of the *Roosevelt*, on this final and successful expedition to the North

Pole, but it was to be a great disappointment for him. On this third trip to Etah, the most northerly settlement in the world, they once more took on an abundance of supplies, including over two hundred dogs and more than sixty tons of whale meat to feed them. Also on board when they left port were seventy-six Inuit men, women and children. One of the tasks of the children in the coming months would be to melt ice and keep a supply of drinking water on hand. Sailing out of Etah, the *Roosevelt* headed northwest across Kennedy Channel to Cape Sheridan on Ellesmere Island, where it would stay for the winter. There was always the danger of rafting ice crushing and sinking the ship, so all supplies were immediately put ashore. The jumping off point for the final trip to the Pole was to be Cape Columbia, 90 miles from here and the most northerly point in North America, about 400 miles from the Pole.

It was now early September, and for the next five months there was to be "heavy traffic" between the two capes, in the form of heavily loaded sleds going to Cape Columbia and empty sleds coming back. A lot of hunting was done that winter also, to build up the supply of fresh meat. There was no problem with refrigeration. With all the supplies at Cape Columbia, Bartlett's job now was to blaze a trail directly to the North Pole which Peary could follow. As before, igloos were built along the way to store supplies, and in one month the last post was established just 150 miles from the final destination. Bartlett would wait here for Peary to arrive, so that they could both make the final "dash "together, as planned. When Peary reached this post, however, much to Bartlett's dismay, Peary ordered him to return to the ship. This is where the controversy begins. There are various theories as to why Bartlett was ordered back:

> 1.   Peary knew there was a possibility of both men being lost, in which case there would be no competent leader to take the Inuit workers back to the ship, or indeed take the ship back to civilization. If this was the real reason, it was a good one, for it took Bartlett and the others eighteen days of

hard going to get back to land. He even fell through thin ice one day and nearly drowned. Fortunately, the accident happened near one of their igloos, and the Inuit were able to rescue him and put him inside and get dry skins on him before he froze to death.

2.   Peary wanted to be the only white man to reach the Pole and did not want to share the glory with anyone else, especially a non-American. He would take fellow explorere, Matthew Henson, an African-American, and the four best Inuit dog sledge handlers, but Peary himself later said" they didn't count because they were Eskimos."

3.   Another reason and the most accepted one by Peary's critics; was that he knew he would probably not reach the Pole, but could claim he did, if he had no competent navigator along to prove otherwise.

It must be remembered that Peary was severely crippled since his first expedition when he lost all his toes, and now had to do most of the traveling on the dog sleds. Navigation in the Arctic is more difficult than anywhere else on earth, mainly because the compass needle points to the magnetic north, which is south of the North Pole and is constantly changing. Navigation has to be done by means of a chronometer (a very accurate watch) and a sextant (an instrument for measuring angles of the sun, in relation to the horizon). A compass is just about useless. Bartlett was a very skillful navigator, and Peary was not. In any event, on April 1, 1901, Bartlett left this last post for the return journey to the ship, and Peary went north with his five men and the same number of dog teams. Bartlett estimated Peary should reach the Pole in eight days, and Peary later claimed he did. Bartlett waited on board the *Roosevelt* for Peary, and was surprised when he got back nearly two weeks earlier than expected. This was the big

Captain Bob Bartlett, world-famous Arctic explorer, grew up in Brigus Newfoundland.

argument used by many scholars and researchers who say it was impossible for him to get to the Pole and back to the ship in such a short time. Bartlett, however, believed him, or said he did, although Peary had no proof, only his word. Strangely enough the diary which Peary kept on the trip disappeared. The editors of *Encyclopaedia Britannica* believed him, too, for in their story on this great explorer, they credit him as being the discoverer of the North Pole. Author Harold Horwood, who wrote the book, *Bartlett: The Great Explorer*, carried out a tremendous amount of research on Peary, and he is convinced that he didn't make it.

Regardless of whether he made it or not, and in spite of the disagreement they had when Bartlett was ordered back, they arrived back in New York good friends, and received a hero's welcome.

Bartlett's Funeral

Captain Bob Bartlett died of pneumonia in New York city on April 28, 1946. He was seventy. His passing was widely publicised in the United States, for he had long ago become an American citizen in order to have easier access to funding for exploring. He was now considered a great American explorer. Although he spent most of his adult "ashore "life in the United States, he always kept in touch with his friends and relatives at home. He wanted to be buried in Brigus after he died. His wishes were carried out, as mentioned at the beginning of this story. The actual wake took place in a large room in his old home, Hawthorne Cottage. On the walls surrounding the casket were numerous testimonials to his fame, as well as many autographed photographs of national and international celebrities.

As the horse-drawn hearse moved away from the home, it was preceded by another hearse banked with floral tributes to the great man. Guards of Honor from the U. S. Scouts and Tasker Lodge 4545, as well as six men who had sailed with the captain, gave the procession the air of a state funeral. Also present were Sir John Puddister, representing the Commission Government, the Chief of Police for Newfoundland, Llewellyn Strange, and members of the American and Canadian Armed Forces. As the procession made its way slowly through the town, the bells of the United, Anglican and Roman Catholic Churches pealed in unison. The final services at the United Church Cemetery were conducted by Rev. George Broughton.

The Sabena Airliner Crash near Gander in 1946

On Wednesday, September 18, 1946, a Belgian transatlantic airliner crashed 25 miles from Gander airport, killing twenty-six of the forty-four people on board. It took three days to get the survivors out of the wilderness.

The Sabena Airlines plane had left Ireland, en route to New York, and was to stop for refueling at Gander. When it reached the airport, it began circling in the total darkness and requested permission to land, as it was running low on fuel. The Gander tower told the plane it could land safely, in spite of poor weather conditions, as they had the very sophisticated "Ground Controlled Approach System," which allows aircraft to be "talked down" in the worst possible weather. This last message was not acknowledged, and whether it was received or not will never be known, as the two pilots died in the crash. What is known is that there were severe magnetic storms in the area, caused by great displays of "Northern Lights," and this phenomenon interfered with radio reception. When repeated attempts to contact the aircraft failed, the tower alerted the Coast Guard, and two hours later when daylight came, several planes searched the area around the airport. One Coast Guard plane searched Bonavista Bay, over which the missing airliner was known to have flown. Soon visibility decreased considerably, and the search had to be called off for the day. In the meantime, the huge "Skymaster" airliner had run out of fuel twenty-five miles south-west of the airport, and glided in to a crash-landing in the woods. The fact that it plowed down trees for a distance of 1500 feet attests to the speed at which the plane was traveling, before breaking up and bursting into flames. Only one of the seven crew members, a stewardess, survived. Seventeen of the thirty-seven passengers lived through the crash with varying degrees of injuries. Nearly all the passengers were businessmen.

During the morning, they heard planes flying about overhead, and were encouraged by this, knowing that at least the searchers were looking in the right area. Very soon, however, the fog came in and their spirits were dampened. All the food in the airliner had been destroyed in the fire, and three or four hours after the crash, three teen-age survivors decided they would try to walk to the airport. From the outset, they were at a great disadvantage, as the three, aged fourteen, sixteen and nineteen, were barefooted, their shoes having been lost in the crash. The fourteen-year-old was the son of the president of Sabena Airlines. As the day wore on, and the weather grew worse, it was painfully obvious that the survivors would have to spend the night in the woods. In the afternoon all the survivors got together (actually for the first time), and sat around a campfire that had been built near the wreckage. The tail section of the plane was not burned out, and they were able to get some blankets and warm clothes from there, and from the luggage that had been scattered about. They made the best of a bad situation.

The next day, Thursday, dawned with fine weather, and as the morning brightened, so did their spirits. They knew they could be easily spotted now. Search planes from Gander and Argentia were already in the air, but this time in a different area.

The survivors had noticed the occasional commercial airliner flying by, en route to the refueling stop, and were disappointed no one had seen them. At 10 a.m. one such plane flew by and then turned around and came back. It circled and flew in much lower this time, and they realized they had been seen at last. Sure enough, a commercial airliner coming from New York, en route to Cairo via Gander, had seen them. The pilot, Captain Ray Jannings, reported to the tower that he saw three people walking around near the crashed plane, which was burned out, except for the tail section, and three more men walking away, about four miles from the site. Within the hour, food, blankets and medical supplies were being dropped by parachute, and a note saying a rescue party was on the way. Indeed, a rescue party of fifteen United States soldiers and medics, led by Captain Samuel Martin, a medical doctor, was already in the air in a Coast Guard flying boat, and was about to set down on a small pond, five miles from the crash site. From there, they would travel up a river in rubber crash-boats, and walk the rest of the way through the forest.

At the crash site, the survivors had not eaten in over twenty-four hours, and were understandably very hungry. However, they had heard about the Newfoundland weather, and fearing it might close in again, rationed the food that had been dropped, so that it would last longer. In the afternoon, two trappers showed up and made some tea, they passed it around. The stewardess had found a silver jug in the ruins of the plane and boiled some water. One of the survivors jokingly asked the trappers, "Do

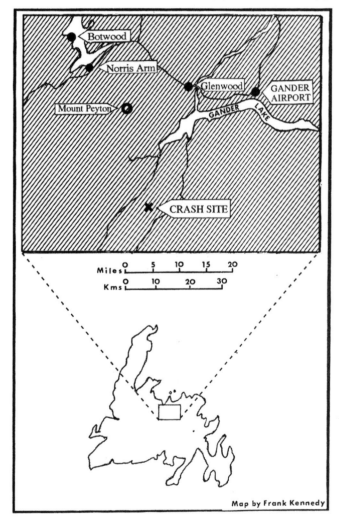

Map shows site of crash, 25 miles south-west of Gander in 1946.
It took three days to get eighteen survivors out of the woods.

you have any lemon?" After a short while, the trappers left, and said they would go and seek help, and would return, but they never did come back. Late in the afternoon, the survivors were thrilled to hear people coming through the brush. "The rescuers!" they thought. Once more they were disappointed, when out of the woods came the three teenagers who had left the day before. The young men had to give up their trek through the wilderness, as one of them was suffering from loss of blood from a severe gash in his hand, as a result of the crash. It was just as well they did turn back, as they never could have made it on foot. The huge thirty-mile-long Gander Lake lay between them and the airport. As darkness began to close in at 7:30 p.m., disappointment turned to despair, and some wondered whether the seriously injured would make it through another night. At 8:30 p.m., as they lay huddled around the fire, they heard a great commotion in the woods, and peering into the darkness in excited anticipation, they were delighted to see men with flashlights and backpacks coming towards them. It was the fifteen man rescue party! The going had been tough, but they were tougher, and they had seen the glow of the fire and homed in on it. At once, the doctor and medics began treating the injured. Several had broken bones, and pain killers were administered where required. Meanwhile, the soldiers set up tents for the night, and everyone was made as comfortable as possible. The soldiers kept a huge fire going all night to warm the area. On Friday morning more supplies, food, blankets and a walkie-talkie were dropped, and at last, communications with the crash site were established. Dr. Martin let it be known that many of the injured could not be moved down the river, and other arrangements would have to be made as quickly as possible. There were no helicopters on the island capable of moving stretcher cases, so in New York, a Coast Guard chopper was partially dismantled and put on board a large airplane and flown to Gander. There it was reassembled, and by Saturday afternoon, the most seriously injured were flown back to the Gander Hospital. Even this was a slow process, as only one patient could be taken out at a time, and when darkness fell, ten survivors would have to spend their fourth night out of doors. On

Sunday they were taken out. Some were well enough to make the trip back down the river with the rescue party, who had finished their work and were now returning to Gander.

Back at the airport, all the survivors had great praise for the U. S. rescue party, especially for Dr. Martin, and they wanted to call the crash site "St. Martin-in-the-Woods" in his honor. In Belgium and in the United States, authorities decided not to take out the bodies of the victims, because such an undertaking would be very dangerous for personnel involved. All twenty-six were buried at the site by a special task force, and as the interments were taking place, funeral services were carried out on board a U. S. Coast Guard plane circling overhead.

The Capitol Theater Fire

On the night of Friday, October 25, 1946, a fire broke out and completely destroyed the very popular Capitol Movie Theater in St. John's, located on Duckworth Street on the third floor of the Total Abstinence and Benefit Society building. The entrance was on Henry Street. The late John O'Brien and I were working in the photography department of the *Daily News* just across the street, when shortly after midnight we heard a fire truck stop nearby. Looking out of a window we saw flames coming from a top window in the west end of the wooden building. The fire was first noticed by a passerby on Duckworth Street, who was startled by glass crashing to the sidewalk in front of him. Looking up, he saw flames coming from the third storey, and sounded the alarm. O'Brien and I took our press camera, and for the next three hours watched and took pictures as firemen battled the blaze.

The fire had started with a cigarette, carelessly dropped on the thick carpet at the rear of the theater during or after the last show, which ended at eleven o'clock. The carpet smoldered for some time before igniting. Then the flames went up a side wall, through the ceiling, and into the huge attic. The attic contained a vast amount of tinder-dry wooden and canvas flats and scenery used years earlier before the building became a movie

TELEPHONE
BUILDING

Capitol Theatre fire rages out of control in downtown St. John's early morning of October 26, 1946. Daily News *Photo by Frank Kennedy.*

theater. It was then known as "The Casino," and was a high-class show-place, where many leading artists and local and foreign companies performed over the years. It was the only theater in the city, besides the "Nickel," that had soft, padded seats. This whole attic was on fire when firemen arrived, and they climbed onto the roof and cut holes to pour water in. It was soon realized by Fire Chief Fred Vivian that the blaze was out of control, and he ordered his men off the roof. No sooner were they back on the ground, than the roof collapsed.

Efforts were then concentrated on saving nearby buildings. Some residents on Henry Street moved furniture out onto the street, when it seemed the fire might spread. Others climbed to their roofs with buckets of water to douse sparks and flankers that fell from the sky. In those days, before dial telephones, several telephone operators were on duty in the top floor of the Avalon Telephone building next door, and much credit was due them for remaining on the job at the height of the blaze. However, when the western wall of the theater burned away, leaving a large chimney unsupported (see photo), firemen thought this could crash through the roof, and police ordered the brave ladies out of the building. Fortunately there was very little wind that night, and using no less than twenty streams of water from hydrants on Henry, Duckworth and Water Streets and Dick's Square, firemen were able to contain the fire in the one building. Flames did eat their way down through the ceiling of the T. A. club-rooms on the second floor, but firemen soon checked this. There was water damage to the club rooms, but firemen managed to cover the expensive billiard tables, trophy cases and other furniture with tarpaulins, thus minimizing this loss. On the ground floor, offices of the Newfoundland Fuel and Engineering Company also had water damage. When the *Daily News* hit the streets at 7:00 a. m., we had the story and several pictures, but firemen were still pouring water on the smoldering ruins of the Capitol, which had been a first-rate movie theater for twelve years. The last picture shown there was *The Killers* starring Burt Lancaster and Ava Gardner. The theater was rebuilt and reopened, but after a few years, with the coming of television to St. John's, attendance dropped off, and it was forced to close once more. It is now owned by the CBC and used for storage.

Movie Theaters in St. John's in the 40s and 50s

In the years before television, moviegoing was a very popular form of entertainment in St. John's. There were nine theaters in the city, each having three shows daily except Sundays, when all were closed. Starting times were 2:00 p. m., 7:00 p. m. and 9:00 p. m. The average run of a full length picture was only three days, but a particularly good movie might be held over for a week. A weekly feature in all the movie theatres was the Newsreel, showing current national and world news events. When an especially important news item would take place, such as an earthquake, or a coronation, the local theaters would sometimes have the pictures as early as two weeks after the event, which at the time was considered unusual. In their newspaper ads they would proudly proclaim, "Special, Exclusive Pictures of the California Earthquake (or whatever event)." In the 1930s, the Little Star Theater on New Gower Street had only one projector, and every twenty minutes there was an interruption in the show, and a slide advertising a coming attraction on the screen, as the reel was being changed. The theaters with location and approximate seating capacity are as follows:

1. The Nickel Theater, first movie house in Newfoundland, in the B. I. S. building, on Queen's Road with entrance and exits on Military Road, eight hundred seats.

2. Capitol Theater, in the T. A. Building on Duckworth Street with entrance and exits on Henry Street, one thousand seats.

3. Paramount Theater on Harvey Road, twelve hundred seats.

4. Cornwall Theater on LeMarchant Road, eight hundred seats.

5. York Theater, formerly The Queen Theater affectionately known as "Johnny Duff's," George Street, entrance on Water Street, exits on George Street, fourteen hundred seats (largest theater in the city). Later destroyed in spectacular fire.

6. The Popular Star on Henry Street, one thousand seats.

7. The Little Star, later renamed The Regal, on New Gower Street, eight hundred seats.

8. The Majestic, on corner of Duckworth Street and Theater Hill (now Queen's Road), seven hundred seats. First city theater to have "sound movies" or "talkies," as they were known in 1929.

9. The Crescent Theater on Water Street, eight hundred seats.

The Paramount Theatre on Harvey Road with twelve hundred seats.

York Theatre in downtown St. John's is destroyed in spectacular fire.
Photo by Frank Kennedy

Other Local News Events for the Year 1946

Jan. 15	Appointment of Sir Gordon MacDonald as Governor of Newfoundland announced.
April 4	*HM.C.S. Wesleyville* launched at Clarenville.
June 17	Devastating forest fire at Glovertown. Fifty buildings destroyed.
Sept. 19	Belgian airliner crashes near Gander Airport killing twenty-nine. Eighteen persons survive.

The Traytown Forest Fire of 1947

In June 1947 a forest fire broke out in central Newfoundland and burned for three weeks. This was before the advent of water bombers, and all fire fighting had to be done from the ground. A first intimation of the seriousness of the fire was when the chief of police in St. John's received a message from Traytown, requesting a steamer be sent there to evacuate the residents. The fire had then been burning a week. (The Newfoundland Constabulary serviced all Newfoundland at that time.) The *S. S. Glenco* was sent to the town and remained there for two days, until it began to rain and the fire died down and all danger seemed to be past. On July 2, bright sunshine and warm westerly winds fanned the embers and an inferno really got started; but the ship was gone by now.

The *Daily News* decided to send me by train to cover the story. Traytown is a few miles east of Glovertown and just west of what is now Terra Nova National Park. No telephone connection in those days, but my first telegram to the Daily News, which was printed verbatim on July 7, gives some idea of the situation at the time:

"Fire completely out of control today. Seventy-five men working with ten pumps. Fire going slowly towards Traytown and is in dense woods on a three-mile front. People left Traytown yesterday after burying their furniture in the ground. Only hope for Traytown is rain or a change of wind, but the latter may endanger Glovertown or South Shore. Fire may reach houses tonight. Forty square miles now burned in Terra Nova and Glovertown fires in last two weeks."

Next day in St. John's, pilot Eric Blackwood of Newfoundland Aero Sales and Service Company advised the *"News"* that he had landed his Sea Bee plane near Traytown and taken on board the *Daily News* photographer and made a survey of the fire area. The plane, one of six operating in Newfoundland by Blackwood's company, was under charter by the Dept. of Natural Resources and on board from that department was Mr. Charles Cahill who invited me up to have a look. From the air we could see a wide area of fire in back of Traytown, but the settlement was hidden from view by a dense pall of smoke. The fire was burning in heavy timber with tongues of flames leaping hundreds of feet in the air and columns of black smoke spiraling skyward. On the ground, men were fighting gallantly to save their earthly possessions; women and children were disconsolate and worried and temporarily bereft of the comforts of their homes; wild life was darting here and there in utter confusion and bewilderment. A rabbit ran out of the woods and stopped ten feet in front of me, as if posing for a picture. I snapped him and then he continued on to safety. A big bear even ambled out of the woods and disappeared down the road in the smoke. The women and children and elderly people were now moved out by car and truck and taken to Glovertown. Only the able-bodied men remained, although much later that day I saw an elderly lady walking slowly away with an armload of clothes. A truckload of men came in from Glovertown to help fight the fire.

Worried mother and frightened son flee their home in June 1947, as huge forest fire threatens Traytown. They had to stay in Glovertown four nights until the fire was under control. Daily News *Photo by Frank Kennedy*

Some put their dories on trucks and moved them up near their houses where they filled the boats with water and stood by with buckets, to douse small fires as sparks and flankers fell around them. I saw a large bathtub filled with water in front of one house. Some men plowed large shallow holes in their fields and put furniture in there. Then they spread tarpaulins over it and covered the tarps with topsoil. The smoke was so thick on the road leading to Glovertown that some car engines actually shut off for want of air and the passengers had to flee on foot. Sixty men with pumps were working at the fire front, and the heat and smoke became so intense that they had to retreat and go back to the individual houses and try hosing them down. These brave men, eyes red from lack of sleep and irritation from the smoke, stood calmly by their homes, peering through the dense blackness for signs of the fire. There was now no way of telling how close the flames really were.

Ambrose Hunter's house was close to the fire, and men with a pump kept dousing it with water. Suddenly the pump broke down. I got a picture of the frantic efforts of the men trying to get the pump started again, and as the picket fence in front of the Hunter home caught fire, the pump did start again and the building was saved. As darkness set in, the ominous red glow became visible about one hundred feet away. By midnight the fire died down, and some of the worn-out men had some well-earned but uneasy sleep. In the United Church School in Glovertown, six miles away, the women and children stayed four nights, sleeping on chairs and on the floor of the gym. They were very grateful to the people of Glovertown who treated them so well in such trying times. Everyone prayed for rain, and on July 9, the prayers were answered when heavy rain began falling and kept coming down for days until the fire was finally out and the residents were able to return to their homes. Although some fences were burned, not one house was destroyed, but financial loss did occur. This fire took place at the height of the logging season and most of the men of Traytown were loggers, but for three weeks they had to stay away from work to protect their homes. And, of course , the dollar value of nearly fifty square miles of destroyed timber is beyond calculation.

The fire started more than ten miles from Traytown on the railway line, probably from sparks from a passing train. At that time all the locomotives burned coal, and sometimes the hot cinders, which were forced out the smoke stack, would start fires. In fact, the usual procedure was for men on "speeders" (four wheeled motor-driven trolleys) to follow along in wooded areas after a train passed through, and put out any fires that occurred. On July 11, the *Daily News* carried the story in two full pages with sixteen photographs.

The Harbour Round Mercy Flight

The *Daily News* described it as "The most thrilling and dangerous mercy flight ever pulled off in Newfoundland history." Not only did we cover the story, we were actually a part of it, when we became lost in the woods on the Baie Verte Peninsula in late October, 1947. So-called "mercy flights" were not common fifty years ago, and when bush pilot Eric Blackwood was asked to go to Harbour Round, to bring back a boy suffering from acute appendicitis, he phoned the *Daily News* and invited a reporter and photographer along to do a story. Chauncey Currie assigned reporter Jack White and myself, and sent us to Quidi Vidi Lake to board Blackwood's seven-passenger Norseman float plane. It was Thursday, October 23, 1947.

Aircraft were allowed to use the lake in those days, and Blackwood had his home base there. His company, Newfoundland Aero Sales and Service, had five other planes flying in Newfoundland at the time. When we arrived at the lake, we were told there would be a delay in the takeoff, as early in the morning strong winds had caused the plane to break its moorings and it had drifted ashore, resulting in slight damage. This might have been an omen of things to come, but repairs were completed by 1:00 p.m., so we took off and headed northwest to the Baie Verte Peninsula. The fourth man on board was Blackwood's mechanic, Jim Collins.

After a short while we were bucking unexpected severe head winds which were tossing the small plane about, and I demonstrated once more that I am not a good sailor, unlike my father, who was a master mariner. I lost my breakfast. Ordinarily, Blackwood would have turned back, but he was thinking of this eight-year-old boy badly in need of hospitalization, so he pressed on. He had been told that the plane could land on Harbour Round, but when we got there, after three hours of rough flying, he flew in and let the plane come down to a few feet above the waves, and decided right away that it was much too rough for a safe landing. Although the plane had a radio, there was no way of communicating with anyone on the ground, so he took the plane

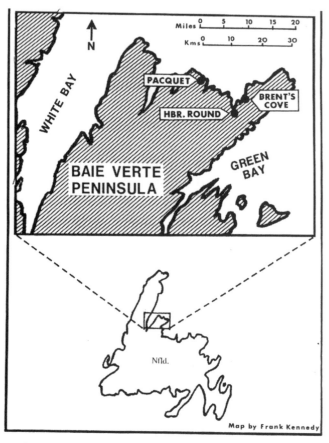

Map shows location of Harbour Round, where sick boy waited to be flown to hospital in 1947.

up and flew out another ten miles to the harbour of Pacquet. This was comparatively calm, being surrounded by hills, and Blackwood and Collins skillfully put the plane down on the water. Two men rowed out in a small boat to see what we were up to. Blackwood told them our problem, and wondered if a boat could be sent the 10 miles to Harbour Round, to bring back the sick boy. We were told that there was no boat large enough in this area to do that in such a rough sea. They suggested that we might be able to land on a large pond about 2 miles inland from Harbour Round, and walk out to the settlement. Blackwood decided to do this.

As mentioned, the harbour at Pacquet was surrounded by hills, which could present difficulties when taking off. On a calm day there would be no problem. We could taxi out into the open sea and have plenty of room, but this was out of the question on that day. Blackwood thanked the men for their suggestion, and as they rowed away, our engine came to life. Blackwood taxied the plane to the very end of the harbour to have as much room as possible for the takeoff. Then he turned the aircraft around into the wind and gunned the motor. Gradually at first the plane picked up speed, and then we were racing along the small waves and quickly using up our takeoff space. We lifted off and directly in front of us loomed a spruce-clad hill. Slowly we gained altitude, and as we hung on to our seats with white knuckles, just managed to clear the trees! Blackwood's skill and good judgment had brought us through. With a great sigh of relief, we headed back to Harbour Round. Once more Blackwood skimmed along over the water, but it was still much too rough to set down. Up we went once more and headed inland over the settlement and located the pond that the Pacquet men had told us about. It was Harbour Round Pond. After first making a low level run just above the surface, to make sure there were no hidden rocks, Blackwood set the plane down and let it drift towards shore. He and Jim Collins climbed out onto the pontoons and secured the craft by tying it up to some trees. Jack White and I then came ashore and thought maybe we should wait around for a while, in case someone came looking for us. The two air-men thought we should walk out to the settlement right away. It was only 2 miles and now only 5:30 p. m. so we should easily make it before dark. Besides, we had had no lunch, and it would be nice to get to Harbour Round and maybe have a cup of tea. The walk would give us an appetite.

Blackwood, obviously prepared for the exigencies of winter travel in Newfoundland, took a tomahawk. Collins took some matches, White took his note pad, I took my camera, and the four of us headed away from the pond, hoping to find a path to the settlement. We found no path, and the going was not easy. No one had overshoes or boots, just dress shoes. At times, walking through bog, we were up to our ankles in mud, and in the woods, small branches near the ground would skin the shins. After walking nearly three hours through woods, across barrens and marshes, we wondered if maybe we were just going around in circles. Our suspicions were confirmed when we came across a boggy area with the unmistakable footprints of four men! Unfortunately, no one had a pocket compass. We plodded on. It was now dark, and to add to our misery, it began to rain. After another three hours we had to admit we were hopelessly lost. We stopped on the side of a gently sloping hill with trees all around, so it was agreed that we may as well spend the night here. Then, at daylight, we could climb to the top of the hill and perhaps get our bearings.

Blackwood and Collins cut some wood and got a good fire going, which was very welcome and badly needed, as our light fall-clothing was soaked through. It rained all night, and we must have been a pitiful sight, standing around the fire with steam rising from our clothes. I took a picture of the three men drying their socks. Although it was raining, we were all quite thirsty, not to mention hungry; and on the side of the hill there were no pools of water we could drink. However, necessity is the mother of invention. The reflector on the flash gun of the press camera was seven inches in diameter, and shaped like a bowl, so I took it off and placed it on a tree stump. Water started collecting in it immediately, so we had plenty of fresh drinking water for the rest of the night. Jim Collins mentioned the emergency rations on board the plane; tins of bully beef, biscuits, etc., and how nice it would be to have some; but of course, there was no way we could find the plane now. I had found a large candy bar in my coat pocket much earlier in the day, but said nothing about it until now. When I produced it, the three other hungry men cried out, almost in unison, "My God, Kennedy, where did you get that?" They almost attacked me as I shared it, one quarter each. This was about midnight, and none of us had had anything to eat since breakfast.

Unknown to us, a ground search party was underway from Harbour Round. Everyone in the settlement knew we were coming, and when they saw the plane go down behind the hills, they waited a couple of hours and when we failed to turn up, feared we had crashed, so eight or ten men went looking for us. They searched all night to no avail. Only once did we hear someone shout "Hello," and we responded at the top of our lungs, but the wind was not in our favor. They never heard us. They even went to Harbour Round Pond and looked along the shore, but the airplane was on the far side and they couldn't see it in the dark. To our horror, before daylight it started snowing, and when dawn did finally come, shortly after five o'clock, visibility was about one hundred feet. That finished the idea of going up to get our bearings. Soon the wind dropped and it became very quiet, with the snow falling on a Christmas Card landscape. This must have been the eye of the storm, for in a few hours the winds were just as bad as ever. However, in the quietness, we could now hear the sound of the sea roaring in the distance, the aftermath of the windstorm the day before, which we later learned was the worst in twenty-eight years. We started walking in that direction, but now the going was more miserable than the previous day, as it was snowing continuously, and we kept sloshing through this in our wet shoes. After a half hour, a happy sight: a path at last! Our spirits were boosted, until a half mile along, when the path ran abruptly right into a pond. Despair! But not for Blackwood. He figured this must be a winter path, where men haul wood to the pond, then across the ice to the other side; and he bet that if we walked half way around the pond, we would find the path again. He was right! We found the path, but it led to another pond. Same thing again. Half way around and another path. Another happy sight; when we continued on past the second pond, we saw a telegraph pole. We knew that if we followed the wire, we would come to a settlement, and the happiest sight of all was at about 8:00 a.m., when, through the snow, we saw the dim outline of houses. We knocked on the front door of the nearest one and waited in anticipation. We could hear children talking inside, so we knocked again. Still no reply. What's happening, we wondered? Why won't they answer the door? Now we knocked harder, and finally a young lady opened the door. She was obviously surprised by what she saw. Four almost exhausted snow-covered men standing there, three with bare heads, their hair matted with snow, and the fourth man wearing a felt hat, with a large camera hanging by his side. When we explained our predicament, she welcomed us into her kitchen. She had heard the day before about the missing men. She apologized that she could offer us nothing but home-made bread and butter and tea. That bread was like manna from heaven. Having had nothing but that one candy bar in the last twenty-four hours, and with all that walking, we were just about starved, and that breakfast was by far the best we ever enjoyed.

The lady was Mrs. William Martin, and she explained that although her young children, Clarence and Mike, heard us at the door, they were afraid to open it. They knew we must be strangers, for none of the local residents would come knocking on the door that early in the morning. She had been upstairs and finally came down. While she was boiling the kettle, Eric told her about the difficult time we had getting here to Harbour Round. "But sir," she exclaimed, "this is not Harbour Round, this is Brent's Cove! " White and I thought, "Good Heavens! Where the heck is Brent's Cove?" She told us that we were 3 miles from Harbour Round and that after we had something to eat, dried our clothes and had some rest, some of her friends would take us back to that settlement. In what seemed like no time at all, the kitchen became literally filled with people. They came to see the men who were lost in the woods all night. Word was immediately sent back to Harbour Round that we were okay, and the search could be called off. After that much appreciated meal, one of the visitors, Mr. Ed Sullivan, took the two flyers to his home, for a few hours sleep. Eric had already announced that the weather was still too bad for a take-off. White and I were taken to the home of Mrs. Jack Sullivan, where we had a few hours of badly needed sleep.

There was a telegraph office in Brent's Cove, but no telephone connection to St. John's, so I sent a message to my mother, explaining my absence. I was not married at that time, and I hadn't bothered telling her about the flight, as we were supposed to be back the same day. In the afternoon, feeling much refreshed, we were escorted back to Harbour Round, and of course, everyone knew where the sick boy lived, so we went straight to his house. Blackwood was worried about his condition, and we were too, especially in view of the further delay in taking off. The boy's name was Eric Aylward, son of Peter, and he didn't seem to be in any great distress. He was being well looked after by a nurse, there being no doctor in the area. She kept applying ice packs and medication to ease his pain. He was still very much in need of the operation, but nothing further could be done that day. Blackwood decided that it was now time to look for our airplane, and we were shown a path that led directly to Harbour Round Pond. Some of the men came along with us, and when we got there, we were surprised to see the aircraft on the other side of the pond. It was covered with snow as was the surrounding countryside, but this was where we had left it on the previous day, and after making sure it was still secure, we walked

Men from Harbour Round took turns carrying a sick boy on home-made stretcher, 3 miles to the waiting plane for the trip to the hospital in St. John's, late October 1947. Daily News *Photo by Frank Kennedy*

back to Harbour Round to spend a much more pleasant night than the first night in this area. Once again we had an outstanding example of Newfoundland hospitality, when the wonderful people of Harbour Round lodged each of us in a different home, in perfect comfort. No one would accept a cent for the food and lodging they so generously gave.

Next morning, at last the weather was good, so we set out to complete our original mission. The men had made a stretcher of "longers" and sail canvas and blankets, and carried the sick boy the three miles to the pond. About a dozen men came along, so they took turns carrying the stretcher along the snow covered path through the woods. At the pond, they carefully put the boy into a small boat and rowed across to the plane. The boy's father, Peter Aylward, was with him all the time. Meanwhile, the four of us walked around the pond, as did some of our hosts, and all arrived at the airplane about the same time. Little Eric was put on board and placed in a position where he could lie down and be as comfortable as possible, as his father sat near him. White and I then got on board after thanking the men for all their kindness, and as we looked at their smiling faces, Jim Collins closed the door and Eric Blackwood started the plane's engine. The pond was calm and mirror-like, and as we took off, we could see the men of Harbour Round waving as they disappeared beneath us.

The flight back to St. John's was very smooth, and took less than two hours. We landed at Quidi Vidi Lake without incident. Blackwood had called ahead from the plane by radio, so there was an ambulance waiting as we arrived. The boy was taken over to the General Hospital, (now the Miller Center) and had immediate surgery. An inquiry by reporter White the next day, would only elicit the information that the patient had had surgery and was doing fine. The caller to the hospital was always asked whether he was a relative, and if not, then no details of the patient's real condition were given.

White and I got back to St. John's on a Saturday, and on the following Monday, the *Daily News* carried a full page story with several pictures. Incidentally, on that same Monday afternoon, the door-bell rang at our home on Patrick Street, and I answered and received the telegram that I had sent my mother three days earlier! Communications have come a long way since then. Many years later, I was speaking with Eric Aylward's uncle, Lester Giles, in Harbour Round, and he informed me that his nephew had been in hospital for an incredible five months. His appendix had ruptured before the operation, and this led to severe complications, so that he could not be released from the hospital until late March of the following year. The story does not end there; although it took three days to get the boy to the hospital, with two actual hours of flight, it took a lot longer for him to get home. Mr. Giles remembered it very well, as it was his own brother who set out with young Eric's father, Peter Aylward, and a dog team from home, and "mushed" all the way to Gander, stopping at various places along the way. At Gander, they picked up the boy, who had come from St. John's by train, and put him on a sled and headed back home, a distance of 150 miles. The round-trip took three weeks!

Other Local News Items for the Year 1947

Jan. 3	Nineteen airliners grounded at Gander because of bad weather in Canada and the United States. (This was before Confederation.)
Jan. 4	It was announced today that UNRRA would buy 50,000 barrels of Newfoundland herring.
Jan. 7	Evening Telegram carriers go on strike for higher remuneration.
Jan. 10	Fire at U.S. Air Base Goose Bay causes two million dollars damage.
Jan. 12	Severe snowstorm halts trains in western Newfoundland.
Jan. 13	Gosse's Woodwork Factory in Spaniard's Bay destroyed by fire.

Jan. 26	Railway vessel *Bonne Bay* ran ashore at St. Shott's. Total loss. All crew saved.
Mar. 5	All Saints Anglican Church, Salmon Cove, Conception Bay, completely destroyed by fire, which was started by lightning.
Mar. 12	St.Patrick's Theater, Bell Island, destroyed by fire.
Mar. 15	Major Peter Cashin sued for libel by Chief Justice, Sir Edward Emerson, Judge Harry Winter, and Court Registrar J. A. Winter.
Apr. 4	Cross country express, *The Overland Limited*, reached St, John's after four day delay, stuck in snow on the Gaff Topsails.
Apr. 17	Jury in Cashin libel suit fail to agree.
Apr. 24	State funeral for Sir John Puddister largely attended.
Apr. 27	*S. S. Eagle* arrives St. John's with 16,700 seals.
May 2	*M. V. Clarenville* arrives St. John's with 8500 seals.
May 4	Banker *Norman Marliyn* ran aground at St. Shott's. Total loss. All crew saved.
May 5	Governor Gordon MacDonald broadcasts to Newfoundlanders from London on BBC.
	Trans Canada Airlines starts Douglas air service from Torbay.

May 9	Delegates from the National Convention express themselves as bitterly disappointed with their reception in London.
May 22	*R. M. S. Newfoundland* launched at Newcastle-on-Tyne.
July 14	Fire on Water Street damages business premises of Dicks & Company and Baine Johnson.
July 17	Evening Telegram ten-mile annual road race won by Pat Kelly. Time: 57 min. 12 sec.
June 19	National Convention delegation leaves for Ottawa.
June 23	New telephone line between St. John's and Bonavista opened.
June24	450th anniversary discovery Newfoundland officially observed.
June 29	United States Army soldier killed near Badger, when army speeder collides with train.
July 19	*S. S. Meigle*, former prison ship, total loss after running aground at St. Shott's.
July 24	*S. S. Amberton*, British freighter, total loss after running aground at St. Shott's.
Sept. 3	Town of Harbour Grace protests against closing of Branch Railway.
Sept. 7	Furness liner, *S. S. Nova Scotia*, arrives in St. John's on maiden voyage from Liverpool England, en route to Boston, Mass. , U. S. A.

Sept. 10   Fishermen returning from the summer Labrador fishery report the fishery was a near failure. Very few schooners had a paying trip.

Sept. 27   F. M. O'Leary, in radio broadcast, out lines the aims of the new Responsible Government League.

Sept. 28   Three St. John's Harbour pilots have narrow escape as their boat was chopped in two by the propeller of a Panamanian steamer.

Oct. 7   Carbonear schooner, *Thos. S. Gorton*, lost near Bonne Bay. Crew saved.

Oct. 17   John Joseph Young of Fishels, charged with murder of Benjamin Webb of Middle Brook.

Oct. 21   Four U. S. servicemen killed in plane crash at Argentia.

Nov. 15   Montreal bound freighter, *S. S. Langlecrag*, runs aground near Sound Island, on northern tip of Great Northern Peninsula. Total loss. forty-one crew members rescued, two lost.

Dec. 17   First oil-burning locomotive for Newfoundland Railway has trial run.

The Hull Home Fire

The most tragic fire that I covered in my forty-two years, in terms of lives lost, was the Hull Home Fire which took thirty-four lives. The date was February 10, 1948, a very frosty winter's day. Hull Home was a three-storey concrete building on the corner of Springdale and New Gower Street in St. John's. It was a nursing home run by Mr. & Mrs. Isaac Hull. Forty-one patients lived there on the second and third floors, and were paid for by the Department of Public Health and Welfare. Eighteen had tuberculosis, eight were mental patients, and the others were very elderly people, some bed-ridden. A seventeen-year-old student, Howard Pike, also lived there, and Mr. Hull spent most nights there, although he and his wife lived in a house on Allandale Road. There was a great demand for this type of accommodation in the late 1940s, so Hull Home expanded to another building to the west. It had twenty-two people living there, with many more on a waiting list. This building was called "The Annex."

On the day of the fire, Mr. Hull arose at 6:45 a.m. and turned on the oil range in the kitchen on the second floor. The oil range was for cooking; heating of the building was by hot water radiation, from a furnace in the basement. After a few minutes, Hull dropped in a lighted match and then went out to the Annex to light the coal stove. A staff of four women were due to come in at 8:00 a. m. When Hull got back to the kitchen in the main building some time later, flames were coming up around the range and the wall behind was on fire. Having no fire extinguishers, Hull rushed to the kitchen sink to fill a bucket with water. Before this was accomplished, however, he was forced out of the room by the flames. Running to the foot of the stairs leading to the third floor, he began yelling that the place was on fire. At the same time, he met the young student, who was already up, and told him to call the fire department. Pike did this from a telephone in the hallway. The young man then started up the stairs in an attempt to help some of the patients, but when he saw Hull leaving, he decided to follow him.

Hull said afterwards that he was afraid to go upstairs to help the patients, because he feared he might be trapped himself. As it was, after a short time standing there shouting, he was forced by the flames to leave the building. Some of the patients on the second floor managed to get down to safety, but the fire quickly engulfed the stairway to the third floor, cutting off that exit. On the sidewalk outside, Hull and Pike were urging people on the second floor to jump from the windows. Two young women did, and the two men caught them. A passerby on his way to work, Walter Carew of Flat Rock, caught Daisy Miller, as she jumped from a second floor window.

Firemen coming down Springdale Street could see the building in flames, with people in the third floor windows. When they got to the scene, they immediately put up ladders and managed to save at least seven people, but four or five had already fallen or jumped out, and were killed when they hit the concrete sidewalk. William Wall lived on third floor, and was awakened by someone shouting, "Fire!" He had often wondered what he would do if the place caught fire. Going into the hallway, he was confronted by heavy smoke and flames coming up the stairway. Quickly he went back into his room and closed the door. Opening the window he saw flames coming from the floor below, and decided to put his plan into action. He grabbed the mattress from his bed and threw it down to the sidewalk below. This, he hoped, might cushion his fall somewhat, in case he did have to jump. His closing the door probably saved his life, as after he'd thrown the mattress out, and before the heat and smoke became unbearable, firemen had a ladder up to the window and he was saved. Twenty-three-year-old Alice Connors lived in a room across the hall from Mr. Wall. She was a tuberculosis patient, having been transferred from the Sanatorium as being incurable. When she became aware of the fire, she awaked other patients in her room, and tried to get them to come over to Mr. Wall's room at the front of the building. She heard a male patient shout, "We're gone this time!" The other patients would not follow her, and soon they were overcome by the smoke and all died in that room. From Mr. Wall's room, Miss Connors was helped down the same ladder used by him, and thus escaped the inferno.

Hector Carter, a *Daily News* printer, was walking to work when he came upon the scene, before the firemen arrived. He was horrified to see a man fall from a third floor window. On the way down, his feet hit a ledge over the first floor of the building, and the body somersaulted, so that he hit the sidewalk head first. Carter believed he died instantly. Another witness was Jean Baird, a teenager who lived across the street. She was awaked by a strong smell of smoke and thought her house was on fire. Jumping out of bed, she ran to the window just in time to see the terrifying sight of several people falling out of the windows across the street, and dying as they hit the sidewalk. It was something she would never forget, and she ran and hid in a room in the back of the house. She was so frightened, that she refused to come out for several hours, until long after the fire was over. Sally Hann also lived across the street. She remembers seeing a young woman jump out of a window, and a man trying to catch her. He couldn't do it, and she crashed to the ground.

As flames shot from the roof, Fire Chief Vivian and District Chief Caddigan feared the Annex might catch fire, so they decided to evacuate that building in spite of the intense frost. It was a wooden building, and firemen were already pouring water on it. Caddigan took two men and tried to enter. They couldn't get in. The panic-stricken residents had barred the door and the firemen had to break it down. The frightened people shied away, but Caddigan managed to calm them, and finally persuaded them to leave for their own safety. They were escorted to various homes in the neighborhood to receive temporary shelter from the bitter cold. Members of the Salvation Army were on hand serving hot coffee to the survivors and firemen. Chief Vivian and Chief of Police Strange both had hands and ears frostbitten, but remained on the job until the fire was out. Vivian even stayed to carry out an inspection of the burned-out building, before seeking medical aid.

When I arrived on the scene at nine o'clock, the fire was just about out, so I first took some photos of the building, with ladders and hoses hanging from the windows, then went inside and photographed firemen searching for bodies among the charred rubble. On being told the victims were being brought to the morgue at the General Hospital for identification, I proceeded there and got shots of bodies being unloaded from a large truck. I had no idea of how many people had died, and it is a pure coincidence that I happen to be writing this story on Tuesday, February 10, 1998, the fiftieth anniversary of that disaster. However, I can still remember the scene that greeted me as I walked into the morgue on this very day, fifty years ago. In the center of the room on a porcelain examination table, lay a broken body partly covered with a white blood-stained sheet. All around on the floor lay seventeen more bodies, most burned beyond recognition; some not much more than blackened skeletons, others with arms missing. One elderly lady had one side of her face looking perfectly normal, while the other side was badly charred. She obviously died in her sleep, lying on her side on a pillow, before the flames reached her. In fact, the autopsy report, done later by Dr. E. Leo Sharpe, stated that all (sic) the victims died of smoke inhalation.

This morgue, not being very large, was literally filled with bodies, and the chapel next door was converted to a temporary morgue. Here sixteen more bodies lay on the floor in similar condition, making thirty-four in total. Grief stricken relatives began arriving in an effort to identify their loved ones. I photographed a gentlemen, hat in hand, near the altar looking for his niece. He couldn't find her. He couldn't be sure any of the bodies was hers. Another white-haired gentlemen, Joseph Milley of Campbell Avenue in St. John's, was trying to locate his fifty-year-old sister. He succeeded. The scene was bad enough for me, a newsman, but for those trying to identify the bodies of loved ones, the experience must have been horrendous.

Less than two weeks later, a judicial inquiry got underway, headed by Justice Sir Edward Emerson of the Supreme Court of Newfoundland. This inquiry uncovered some startling facts. The unbelievable buck-passing that occurred during the previous eighteen months was undoubtedly a great contributing factor to such a large loss of life. In 1946, nearly two years before the fire, a routine inspection of the home was carried out by City Building

Inspector F. M. Cahill and Fire Chief Fred Vivian. In their report they made some strong recommendations regarding the building:

1 An outside fire escape should be installed at the rear of the building.

2. A fire shield should be placed on the wall in the kitchen, behind the oil range (they had seen scorch marks on the wall).

3 The range should be checked immediately and a new carburetor installed.

4. All exit doors should open outwards (they opened inwards).

The inspectors also objected to the narrowness of the stairways, which were only thirty inches wide in some places. Copies of this report were sent to the St. John's City Council, the chief of police, and the Department of Public Health and Welfare. The latter department then made an independent inspection, but took no further action. They sent the original report back to the City Council, claiming no responsibility in the matter, and suggesting the Council should send the report to Mr. Hull. This was not done.

Hull was asked about this at the inquiry. Emerson wanted to know who had sent him the report. Hull replied that no one had sent him a report, and he first learned of it when he read about it in the newspapers. Asked why he didn't act on the recommendations, he said he had heard nothing from the Public Health Department after their inspection. Since they kept sending him new patients, he assumed that they were satisfied with the condition of the nursing home. Testimony of several oil-burner mechanics showed a long history of trouble with the stove. One witness, Graham Whitten, said someone had tied down the trip valve in the carburetor to keep it open. This allowed a lot more oil than normal to flow into the stove. He had warned Hull that it was dangerous to tamper with the carburetor. Mr. F. G.

Wylie, who occupied the ground floor of the building, testified that several months earlier, the stove was leaking so badly, oil was dripping down through his ceiling, and he had to move goods and put a pan underneath to catch the fluid. Surprisingly, the inspectors' report did not recommend fire extinguishers or other fire fighting equipment. When asked why he had no fire extinguishers, Hull replied that it never occurred to him that the place might catch fire. The inquiry also found that although the exterior walls were concrete, all the interior construction was wooden, and as the walls and ceilings had been recently painted, this would have accelerated the progress of the fire. Crown Prosecutor Harry Carter could not understand how the City Council had the power to enforce the recommendations, yet failed to do so. Justice Emerson was amazed too, that the Department of Health would deny responsibility, and send the report back to the City Council.

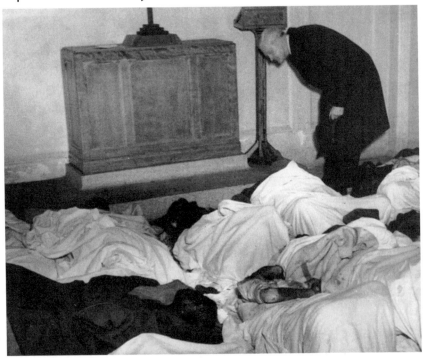

A city resident tries to identify the body of his niece who died in the fire. Daily News *Photo by Frank Kennedy*

At the end of April, 1948, the judge released his findings, and in no uncertain terms, placed the blame for the tragedy on three parties: the Hulls, the St. John's City Council, and the Department of Public Health and Welfare. The actual cause of the fire was the condition of the oil range, due to the negligent conduct of Isaac Hull. The large loss of life was mainly due to understaffing and the absence of a fire escape. The City Council was negligent in failing to ensure the inspectors' recommendations were carried out. The Department of Public Health failed to seek, from higher authority, permission to provide a remedy, either by bearing the expense of a fire escape, or reimbursing the Hulls for doing so. Mr. Emerson praised the conduct of seventeen-year-old Howard Pike, who, after having called the fire department, attempted to make his way upstairs to rescue some patients. The judge felt that Pike would have stayed and helped in the evacuation of residents, if some responsible leadership had been shown.

The former Hull home as it stands today. *Photo by Frank Kennedy*

Today, fifty years later, the concrete walls still stand, and the interior has been rebuilt into office space. On this anniversary day, the Newfoundland CBC supper hour news program, "Here & Now," aired a fine feature on the disaster. Included were interviews by some still living retired firemen who had fought the blaze, as well as this writer and Ms. Sally Hann. In his closing remarks, reporter Jay Callanan made a sad but true observation. Standing before the building, as it exists today, Callanan lamented, "As for the people who perished, they are forgotten. There's nothing, not so much as a plaque to mark the tragedy, or tell anyone they even existed."

Other Local News Items for the Year 1948

Jan. 7	Terra Nova Aviation training-plane crashes near Gander Airport. Evan Boyd and William Rendell seriously injured.
Jan. 16	Newfoundland government presents gift of furs to Princess Elizabeth.
Jan. 17	Schooner *Earle Monsport* of Carbonear sinks at sea. All crew saved.
Jan. 18	Pan Am Airways makes record flight Gander to Shannon, Ireland: 5 hrs., 3min. 393 mph.
Feb. 5	Newfoundland schooner *Ethel M. Petite* lost near Halifax, N. S. Crew of twenty-eight Newfoundlanders all saved.
Feb. 7	Petition for Economic Union with United States launched
Feb. 14	Severe storm hits city. Wind, snow and rain. Side blown out of house on Codner's Lane

Feb. 15	Severe storm at Grand Bank. Three bankers driven ashore. *Isabel L. Corkum* total loss.
Feb. 18	New Railway steamer, *S.S. Springdale*, arrives from Scotland for Green Bay Service.
Feb. 28	Great Eastern Oil Company's store on Water Street destroyed by fire. $200,000 damage.
Mar. 5	First sealing ships leave for the icefields.
Mar. 9	Sealing vessel *J. H. Blackmore* lost near Cape Bonavista. All crew saved.
Mar. 28	First sealer arrives in St. John's. *Linda May* brought back 10,924 pelts.
Mar. 30	Sealing ships *Lady Cecil* and *Bronco and Magdalene* arrive in St. John's.
Apr. 1	Sealing ships, *Terra Nova*, *Eagle* and *Wimoda* arrive.
Apr. 10	Sealing ship, *North Voyager,* arrives with 14,700 pelts.
Apr. 18	Railway new ship, *S. S. Bar Haven* arrives in St. John's.
Apr. 28	United States government announces it will spend $18 million on bases in Newfoundland
Apr. 29	*M. V. Administratrix* sinks when cut in two by Norwegian ship *Lovdal* off Cape Race. Five drowned.
June 6	Danish freighter strikes iceberg 30 miles from St. John's.

Sept. 13	L. S. P. U. strike at Newfoundland Coal Co. premises. Dispute over reduction in number of men used to discharge ships.
Sept. 15	After forty-seven years, street car service ends in St. John's. Buses take over.
Sept. 16	Heavy rainstorm hits St. John's. One person killed as home wrecked on Southside.
Sept. 21	Greek ship *S. S. Orion* wrecked and burned at Flower's Cove. Ten badly burned.
Sept. 28	Portuguese vessel *Marie Joanna* runs aground at Fogo Harbour entrance. Total loss.
Oct. 24	Golden Jubilee Mount Cashel observed.
Oct. 27	*S. S. Ilex,* A. Wareham & Sons, destroyed by fire at Fermeuse.
Nov. 11	New radio transmitter at Wesley United Church officially opened by Rev. Dr. Joyce.
Dec. 1	Five city firemen injured when truck skids into car.
Dec. 1	Fire destroys Grand Bank schooner *M. & L. Lodge*, 45 miles off Cape Breton. Crew of six rowed ashore.
Dec. 23	Grand Bank schooner, *Marion Mosher*, destroyed by fire thirty miles off St. Pierre. Crew all safe. Rowed ashore.

Chapter Three: Lighter Days At The *News*

The "April Fool's Day" Photos

When we were kids, we always enjoyed playing "April Fool" jokes on our friends, and sometimes even on strangers. The tradition seems to be dying out now, but I remember one day when my best friend Jack Brown and I were walking to school on April 1. Near Wesley Church on Patrick Street, we approached an elderly clergyman walking along with a cane. As he passed us, my young friend pointed to the ground behind him and said, "You dropped something, Sir." The minister stopped, turned around and said, "Where?" Jack Brown cried out, "April Fool!" I was amused, but the minister was horrified at this disrespectful prank by a young boy. He reacted swiftly. Swinging around, he lashed out at the boy's backside with his walking cane, at the same time muttering, "You little brat!" I never forgot this incident, and I guess Jack remembered it as long as he lived. Many years later, at the *Daily News*, in 1948, I thought it might be fun to try and fool some of our readers.

The first attempt was a photo of the Colonial Building in ruins, having supposedly collapsed during the night. I had carefully cut up a photograph of the building into small pieces: the pillars, the walls, and the roof, pasted the pieces together to form a pile of rubble. Then I re-photographed the whole mess and we printed it with the heading "Colonial Building Collapsed, No One Injured."

That was the beginning of a series of April 1 fake photos that for the next fifteen years would sometimes fool, sometimes enrage, and sometimes amuse many of our readers. This was long before television came to Newfoundland, and most people were not accustomed to photos portraying something that had not really happened. This first picture was printed on an inside page of the paper, but the boss, Chauncy Currie, liked the idea so much, that all the others were printed on page one.

I would usually try to pick a subject that was then in the news. For instance, when an unidentified flying object was reportedly sighted over the city in March, 1950, we had a photo of two flying saucers streaking over Duckworth Street. When the ferry *William Carson* was damaged by ice on a trip to Labrador in March 1957, she headed back to St. John's for repairs. This had been widely reported in the media, so we had the liner sunk in the Narrows on April 1. She didn't quite make it to the drydock. And when the city bus drivers were trying to get a new contract with the company in 1963, everyone knew about this, so we had a photo of the bus garage, filled with buses, and the heading,

First in a series of "April Fool Photos" showed Colonial building in ruins, having collapsed during the night. This was in 1948. *Photo by Frank Kennedy*

"City Bus Strike Starts Today."

We usually had a fairly plausible explanation for the unusual accident or incident. In 1955 we had a startling picture of Water Street West, near Victoria Park, flooded with six feet of water. The caption noted that hundreds of telephone poles stored on the bank of Waterford River, near Syme's Bridge, had slipped into the river and were swept along by the current. When they came to the railway trestle, where the river is narrow, a huge log-jam occurred and the water backed up and flooded the street. In 1954 we had a photo of a large airliner that had crashed on the football field in front of the (then) Memorial University on Parade Street (now a parking lot). Again we explained that the American National Airlines plane, (no such airline existed) was en route to Gander from London when engine trouble caused it to lose altitude rapidly. The pilot tried to make it to Torbay Airport, but as he swung in over Signal Hill, he knew this would not be possible. In the early morning light, he spotted the large Memorial field and headed down into it. As the landing gear touched down, the left wheels dug deep into the soft ground, flipping the aircraft around and snapping off a wing. One of the engines partly buried itself, but fortunately the plane did not catch fire.

So as not to shock readers, we always made sure to mention early in the story, that no one had been injured. The first line of this plane crash story read, "Thirty-four persons escaped injury at dawn this morning when an American National Airlines plane crash landed, etc" We always had a long caption under the picture. This was a sneaky attempt to have the reader not reach the bottom line, which would reveal the hoax. We hoped they would stop reading all the details, and rush out to the scene to see it for themselves. This is what often happened. In the plane-crash story we even had the caption continued on page three, and it was there that the joke was finally revealed. In the Water Street Flood story, we stated that the water was expected to keep rising "...till noon today, which will give readers plenty of time to find out that this is nothing but an April Fool joke, and our photographer, Frank Kennedy, is at it again."

In 1958 "Sink Holes" were in the news. These were occurring on the mainland, usually the result of underground mining being carried out too close to the surface. Sometimes the earth would cave in and leave large, so-called "sink holes" in the ground. On April 1, we showed the result of the railway station falling into one of these, as the earth underneath the building gave way. The picture showed the station at an awkward angle, half submerged in the ground. Again the plausible explanation. Over the years, the nearby Waterford River had eaten away the ground under the railway station, until the surface collapsed. The caption went on, "As the building slowly sank last night, it formed a hole in the ground almost circular in shape—the same shape as the O's in the words April Fool."

Strangely enough, the most preposterous photo was the one most remembered. This was known as "The Ship Up In Bowring's Cove." I mean, how could a steamer possibly plow up two hundred feet of Bowring's Cove? Absolutely absurd! Yet some readers saw and believed. That was in 1952. I concocted this one with the aid of three separate photographs. A photo of Bowring's Cove, which I took a few days earlier, a photo of a steamer that happened to be tied up in the harbour, and an old photo of an accident that I'd taken years earlier when a truck overturned on Patrick Street. Of course, I put a new name on the ship. Combining the three, the heading read, "Steamer Overturns Truck in Freak Accident." The caption:

> "Early this morning as the S. S. Loof Lirpa was turning around in the harbour, the telegraph mechanism connecting the bridge with the engine room got out of order, with the indicator in the engine room on "Full Ahead." At nearly twenty knots, the steamer plowed straight into Bowring's wharf, and the terrific momentum of its four thousand tons carried the ship some 200 feet up Bowring's Cove, where it hit and overturned a stake-body truck which had

just stopped at the head of the cove. No one was hurt in the unusual accident although the keel tore up pavement and dug a ten foot deep ditch in the cove. Port authorities are wondering how they will get the ship back into the water, but if you will just read the ship's name backwards, you will probably arrive at a solution yourself."

"Loof Lirpa" spelled backwards of course, is April Fool. We had a lot of reports of people not reading all the caption, but going down to Water Street and being somewhat irked to find they had been fooled. The best story came to me a week later, when I happened to meet a bus driver who ran a route early

Best remembered fake photo was the "Ship up in Bowring's Cove" in 1952, where name of steamer spelled backwards was clue to the joke.

every morning from Carbonear to St. John's. The *Daily News* was delivered to Carbonear by 8 a.m. and he had seen the photo and read the complete caption. When the bus came around to Harbour Main, the driver spotted an elderly lady whom he knew waiting at the bus stop. As she got on board he asked, "Well, Mrs. Furey (not her real name), you're going into St. John's today?" "Yes sir," she replied, "I haven't been in the city for ten years, but I'm going in to see the big accident." "What accident?" the driver asked." Oh, the big accident on Water Street where the ship came up Bowring's Cove. Didn't you see the picture in the paper this morning?" she replied. The driver asked the lady whether she had read the caption, and she said she hadn't, because she couldn't read, but she recognized Bowring's Cove and was going in to see it. When he tried to explain that it was only a trick photo, she would have none of that, and yelled, "Why don't you want to take me in? Are you afraid I can't pay? I have money! Here, take it!" (It was the custom then, to pay as you left the bus.) After much more discussion, and with the help of other passengers, she finally began to doubt the validity of the photo, and was persuaded to go back home. But she was not at all happy. I'm glad I never met that lady!

The picture that probably upset most readers was the bus strike shot. I went to the bus garage a day earlier and took a photo of the front of the building, with just one door open, and the front of a bus showing. All the other doors, about a dozen, were closed. When I developed the picture I made ten extra prints, and carefully cut out the open door with the bus in all these prints. Then I glued all these onto the doors in the original photo, so that now it looked as if the garage was completely filled with buses. The heading read, "City Bus Strike Starts Today" and the caption:

> *"A lot of walking will be done by St. John's residents, as a surprise strike of the bus drivers, which may last several weeks, brings all city transportation to a halt today. The company's garage, above, is filled with idle buses as a result of a breakdown in negotiations*

between the union and the company. The fact that the strike may last several weeks will be a severe blow to many citizens, especially those without cars who live a long distance from their place of work. To those of our readers who will be in any way affected by the strike, we can only say very quietly, "April Fool." There will be no strike at all."

As I mentioned above, many readers were upset. The *Daily News* was usually delivered to many city homes by 8 a. m., and in some cases, people who used the buses to go to work, saw the headline and took off to walk to work, some without breakfast. As they hurried along, the bus passed them by. That was the last in the series, as I left the *News* the following year to join the CBC. Maybe it was just as well, before I got myself into some serious trouble. But it was a lot of fun, and my boss, Chauncy Currie,

In March 1957, the ferry *William Carson*, was actually damaged by ice on a trip to Labrador, and was reported to be coming back to St. John's for repairs. Our April 1 photo showed that she didn't quite make it, but sank in the Narrows.

enjoyed it too. Every year, towards the end of March, he would ask me if I had something for April 1. When I said I did, and began to tell him about it, he would always stop me and say, "Don't tell me, I want to be surprised." I liked that. As the years passed, of course, less and less readers were fooled, and instead, many people wondered what the *Daily News* would run each April 1. Other pictures included "City Bus Goes Over Job's Wharf"; "Freight Train Wrecked As Waterford Bridge Trestle Collapses" ; and "Spectacular Pile-up Occurs as Rennies' Bridge Collapses".

More Fun at the News: "Twilight In Yachau"

In the early 1950s the *Daily News* ran an art competition, in which amateur artists were invited to submit paintings. Cash prizes were given each week for the three best works submitted. Black and white pictures of these were published with short write-ups. One day I happened to be in the show-card department of Ayre & Sons on Water Street. This office had three full-time artists painting large price tags, "Sale" signs and posters, for use all around the three-storey department store. The manager there, Charlie Peet, was just putting the final touches on a show card and he asked me about the art contest. He wanted to know who did the judging and I told him the judges were a reporter and an advertising salesman, and I wondered out loud why he had asked. He replied, "Boy, oh boy! They might be good at writing news stories or selling advertising, but they sure don't know much about art." Having finished his show-card, he wiped off his brush with a piece of rag, and threw the latter on the desk at which I was sitting. "Here," he joked, "Why don't you enter this? It's as good as some of the stuff that we see published."I picked up the piece of cloth and looked at it. It had obviously been used to clean many brushes, and was a mess of unrelated blobs of color. Putting it in my pocket, I said, "Yeah, maybe I will." Back at the office, I cut a rectangle out of the odd shaped piece of rag, and glued it to a piece of matte board. I had to consider a title, so I thought "Twilight in Yachau" would be original. Then I came up with a fictitious artist's name, "Woo Tong," I didn't know if this was actually a Chinese name at all, but it sounded as if it might be. My co-worker, the late John O'Brien, agreed. The only thing that was added to the "art work" was two initials, W. T., in the bottom corner. It was beginning to look interesting, but we thought it would add authenticity to the work if we had some Chinese writing as well as the English title. I looked in the *Encyclopaedia Britannica* and found several examples of Chinese writing, and copied down a couple of characters on the matte board. To John and me they really looked like a good example of Chinese writing, but the actual translation in English was, "To eat a horse." No matter. We wrapped up the "painting" and enclosed a note saying, "I live on Bell Island and would like to enter my painting in your art contest. I call it 'Twilight in Yachau' [signed] Woo Tong ". Then we addressed the package, and that evening after the business office had closed, (we had keys, of course) we put it on the reception desk.

That was Monday. Winners were always announced on Thursdays, and on Wednesdays, the three winning paintings would be sent up to our department, where John O'Brien would make photo-engravings. When the three paintings arrived that week, we were astounded to find that "Twilight in Yachau" was declared the first prize winner. I looked at John and asked, "What are we going to do now?" John replied, "Nothing! I'll make the plates and send them down to the composing room as usual." In the newspaper the following morning, the caption read," This week our first prize goes to Woo Tong of Bell Island, for his fine abstract painting, which has to be seen in its true colors to be really appreciated." Then the unbelievable happened. A cheque for the first-prize money was sent out, addressed to Mr. Woo Tong, Bell Island, Newfoundland. By a remarkable coincidence there happened to be a family named Tong on the island! However, they had several young children, but no "Woo Tong", and they sent the cheque back, saying none of them had entered any art contest. A week passed and Charlie Peet of Ayre's could contain himself no longer. He phoned Chauncy Currie, my boss, who was a friend of his, and said, "You pulled a beaut on the art page last

"Twilight in Yachau' fooled the art contest judges.

week!" Currie asked what he meant, and Peet explained that the winning entry was a piece of rag he used to clean his brushes. Unfortunately, he added, "Frank Kennedy knew about that."Currie slammed up the receiver and told his secretary to get Kennedy down to his office right away. I must admit, that in the twenty years I worked at the news, this was the only time he was angry with me. The first thing he said was, "I understand you knew the winning entry in last week's art contest was a hoax?" I admitted I did. I think if he had known that I had actually sent it in, he would have fired me on the spot. He thought Charlie Peet had submitted it, and that I knew about it, but said nothing. He gave me a dressing down, saying how embarrassing it was to send the prize to Bell Island, and how the Tongs were very indignant about it. He said in no uncertain terms that a joke is a joke, but I should have stopped it before it went into print. He impressed on me that nothing like this was ever to happen again. And it didn't. But one thing it did prove: Charlie Peet's assessment of the competence of the judges was correct.

Even More Fun. . . But Dangerous, Maybe!

Murle Chafe came with us as a photographer in the early 1970s and was quite a character. He was a whiz at chemistry, and was delighted to find that we used iodine crystals in our photo-engraving process (not to be confused with the antiseptic tincture of iodine, which is made by dissolving these crystals in alcohol). Murle showed us how to mix iodine with ordinary household ammonia and make a very unstable explosive. True! We would mix only a small amount at a time, and it would form a brown mud. Then we would take tiny portions, smaller than a match head, and throw them out our third-floor window on Duckworth Street. When the mud dried, after a few minutes, the mixture was so unstable that the least bit of friction would set it off. Sometimes even a heavy wind would detonate it. *Encyclopaedia Britannica* says iodine combines with aqueous ammonia to form nitrogen tri-iodide, which is highly explosive! We would enjoy watching cars go by and slow down, sometimes even stop, as a loud bang erupted from under the tires. It was really not too dangerous, as there was no fire or spark with the detonation, just a small flash of purple vapor. There was not even any heat generated. The sound was much like traditional firecrackers. I suppose these are not available today any more.

One day John O'Brien, Nels Squires and myself climbed onto the roof of Bon Marche, a Water Street business adjoining the *Daily News* property to the rear of our building. We knew a parade was due, so we flicked down a few bits of this mud and waited. In less than half an hour, we saw and heard the parade coming up Water Street. It was led by a man on a white horse, and as the animal trotted on the mix, there was a loud report and the horse reared up on its hind legs, almost throwing the rider, Eric Pomeroy, who held on for dear life. He was a good horseman and managed to calm the animal. The very loud sound from the leading band covered up most of the noise of our fireworks, so there was no further disruption of the parade. We took off back to the News building before we were spotted.

A week later, we were at it again, but this was to be our last time, as things started getting out of hand. It was a Wednesday afternoon, a half-holiday in those days, and not much traffic about. Again we threw several little bits out onto Duckworth Street and onto the sidewalk. We must have used a bit more that usual, because when a city bus passed by there was quite an explosion and the driver slammed on the brakes. Getting out of the bus, he was met by two men from the telephone company building, just down the street, who had come out to investigate the noise. As they walked across the sidewalk, they stepped on some iodine-mix and nearly jumped out of their shoes. The bus driver inspected all his tires, and after some discussion with the telephone men, drove away. The latter walked up and down the sidewalk, and there were several more loud reports before they hurried into the building. A few minutes later, a big telephone company linesmen's truck pulled up amid more loud noises, and two men got out. They were immediately joined by the first two men who again exited their building. Another short discussion followed, and then, to our dismay, they started roping off the street. We had to do something now, before the police were called.

Putting my head and shoulders out the third floor window, I shouted to the men these explosions were not dangerous, that some boys had spread some chemicals around the ground earlier. They were not at all convinced, they pointed to several cracks in the concrete sidewalk and shouted back, "Look, the sidewalk is cracking up!" I told them that these were old cracks that had been there for months; and indeed this was so. I continued telling them that I had seen this thing before, and it was just some kind of practical joke, but not dangerous. "Are you sure?" they insisted. "Yes, absolutely!" I replied. Much to our relief, they took down the rope, coiled it up and threw it in the back of the truck. By now all the iodine had gone off anyway, and the street was back to normal. John O'Brien, Nels Squires and I took off for home as fast as we could. Merle Chafe went to the mainland a few years later and we lost track of him, but he was quite a clever guy, with a great sense of humor.

1949: Confederation Year

Newfoundland became Canada's tenth province in 1949, but Newfoundlanders had been seriously considering joining the other provinces even before they got together and formed the Dominion of Canada in 1867. In fact, two delegates from the Newfoundland government attended a conference in Quebec in October 1864, to discuss the union of "Upper Canada" with Quebec, New Brunswick, Nova Scotia, P. E. I. and possibly Newfoundland. The delegates, Frederick Carter and Ambrose Shea, made several suggestions which were agreed to by the conference, but the two had been instructed not to make any commitments regarding Newfoundland, which was under Responsible Government since 1855. When they returned and laid out the terms of the proposed union, the government, under Hugh Hoyles, thought that the matter should be brought before the people of Newfoundland. A referendum was not held, however, and in the following year a coalition government was formed with F. B. Carter as prime minister and the issue was shelved.

Two years later, in 1867, the provinces united to form the Dominion of Canada. This union was allowed under the British

North America Act, passed by the parliament of the United Kingdom earlier that year. Newfoundland remained a colony of Great Britain. In 1869, Newfoundland Governor Anthony Musgrave, suggested that the government should once more consider union with Canada. After much debate, terms were drafted by the House of Assembly, and actually passed by the Canadian Parliament. Prime Minister Carter decided to call an election on the issue to see how the people felt. St. John's businessman Charles Fox Bennett was very much against Confederation and carried out a strong campaign, especially in the outports, stating we would be selling our country to Canada and would have to pay heavy taxes if we joined. His campaign succeeded. When the election was held in November, 1869, only nine of the thirty members elected were in favor of Confederation. So that ended that attempt.

Nearly twenty years later, informal talks were on again, and in 1888 the Canadian Governor-General, the Marquess of Lansdowne, requested a delegation come to Ottawa to once again discuss Confederation. A delegation was formed in the House of Assembly and was scheduled to leave for Ottawa in June, but there was much disagreement among the individual members. Not only could they not agree on some of the proposed terms of union, but some were not even sure they wanted to join Canada at all! With all the arguments going on, the trip was postponed indefinitely. All Newfoundland suffered from the effects of the great fire of 1892 which destroyed most of the city of St. John's, and with the infamous bank crash coming two years later, the colony was in desperate financial straits. In 1895, the Governor, John O'Brien, asked the Governor-General of Canada to once more open talks on Confederation. He agreed, and in April, 1895, a conference opened in Ottawa with an eight member delegation from Newfoundland in attendance. After nearly two weeks, no agreement on the financial arrangements could be met and talks broke down. Canada was not willing to give Newfoundland the money necessary to operate its provincial services, and Great Britain was asked to come up with the balance required, but that request was refused. Back in St. John's, Sir

Robert Bond managed to obtain substantial loans from Montreal and London, and so the country was saved from bankruptcy. For many decades the people remembered that Canada would not help Newfoundland when help was so badly needed, and so nobody wanted to consider Confederation for years to come.

Commission Government

On February 16, 1934, the Newfoundland government, under Fred Alderdice voluntarily dissolved the House of Assembly in favor of a recommended Commission Government, consisting of three appointed members from Great Britain, three from Newfoundland and the present Newfoundland Governor. These seven men were to run the country until it became:

Colonial Building in St. John's, site of the National Convention, 1946 - 1948.

"... financially stable and Responsible Government was requested by the people..."

After twelve years that desirable state was reached, thanks to, amongst other things, the establishing of American, Canadian and British military bases on the island and in Labrador during the second World War.

The National Convention

On June 21, 1946, for the first time in 14 years, Newfoundlanders went to the polls. They were not voting for a new government, however, but for forty-five members of a National Convention to consider and discuss the future of Newfoundland, and to make recommendations to the United Kingdom. Voter turnout was low and eight of the candidates were unopposed. Most of the elected members had no previous political experience and none expressed publicly any particular political leaning. The convention opened on September 12th, 1946, in the Colonial Building in St. John's, and we covered many of the sessions for the *Daily News*. It soon became obvious that most of the forty-five members were against the present form of Commission Government. Those in favor of Confederation were led by Joey Smallwood. The pro-Responsible Government group had Major Peter Cashin as their fiery leader. In October, Joseph Smallwood made a motion to send a delegation to Ottawa to discuss Confederation. The motion was defeated after the urging of Major Peter Cashin. Nevertheless, four months later, a similar motion was carried.

Before going to Ottawa, however, it was decided to send a delegation to London to find out what help Britain would give Newfoundland, if the people wanted to go back to Responsible Government. Smallwood declined going along because he already secretly knew what the outcome would be. He was right. Britain would give no financial help to Newfoundlanders, unless they decided to keep Commission Government, and Smallwood knew too, that this was the last thing the people wanted. The delegation's visit to London in the winter of 1947 was a short one, unlike the trip to Ottawa, which lasted all the following summer. Both delegations were led by Gordon Bradley, chairman of the National Convention, a strong Confederate, but he was working hand in glove with Smallwood, who did go to Ottawa. Canadian Prime Minister MacKenzie King liked the idea of rounding out the country from "sea to sea" during his reign, but he was not prepared to grant any concessions to Newfoundland that were not already available to the other provinces. He made this clear to the head of the Canadian delegation, Louis St. Laurent, minister for external affairs and to the other eight ministers on the Canadian committee.

The arguments dragged on and on, and it became painfully obvious that the Newfoundland delegation had no power to make decisions regarding negotiations. Back at home, the Convention was at a standstill and many members, and indeed many Newfoundlanders were wondering why the delegates were staying away so long. Many felt they were having a paid holiday. The Responsible Government group had had enough, and decided in private meetings to call for the impeachment of Chairman Bradley as soon as he returned. Smallwood and Bradley heard about this while still in Ottawa, and came up with their own plan to thwart the censure. When the delegation returned in the fall, the National Convention reconvened, and at the first session, the public galleries were filled with media people and spectators in anticipation of what was expected to happen. Chairman Bradley, looking very stately, called the meeting to order and introduced the first speaker, Joey Smallwood. Mr. Smallwood, uncharacteristically, was very brief, explaining that the actual terms of union would be tabled later. As he sat down, Bert Butt stood up. He was a staunch Responsible Government supporter and had been chosen to move the vote of censure. As Butt uttered his first words, "Mr. Chairman," Bradley slowly rose to his feet and very calmly interrupted with, "Just a moment, Mr. Butt, if you please." Butt attempted to continue but Bradley repeated the request and Butt sat down. For a moment there was absolute silence, then Bradley, with his loud, impressive voice, berated all those who had criticized his work in Ottawa, and carried on with a tirade against those who questioned his personal integrity. After another brief pause, as if to let the words sink in, Bradley looked around at all the very attentive faces and stated dramatically," Gentlemen, this convention is without a chairman! "With that he walked out of the chamber. It is unfortunate there were no television cameras in those days to record the bedlam that followed. Smallwood triumphantly jumped to the center of the room and shouted,"Where do we go from here boys?" Shouts of," Order!, Order!" came from the floor, and Smallwood shouted back,"What Order'?" We can't do anything, we haven't got a chairman!" Some members, now riled up, rushed unto the floor with clenched fists, to physically attack him, and had to be restrained. Such shouting and cursing had never been heard in the Colonial Building since the riot of 1932.

When the furor finally died down, Convention Secretary Gordon Warren took the chair, and it was decided to ask the government to appoint a new chairman. When sittings resumed on October 15, Mr. J. B. McEvoy, a prominent St. John's lawyer, was in the chair. Bradley took his place as an ordinary member and received no further criticism. The Convention now got down to the serious business of discussing the various forms of government. Smallwood and Cashin were highly skilled debaters, and they fought tooth and nail, each hammering home the advantages and disadvantages of Confederation. All forty-five members got to express their opinion and as they were aware that the entire proceedings were being broadcast live on radio, many of the views were in the nature of campaign speeches. The Convention was to recommend to the United Kingdom which forms of government the people of Newfoundland should be asked to choose from. After an all-night session in January, 1948, by a vote of 29 to 16, Confederation was not recommended. The word sent to the U.K. was that the people should have two choices: Commission Government or Responsible Government. Having fulfilled its mandate, the National Convention closed on January 30, 1948.

Although the Confederates were unsuccessful at the convention, they began a strong lobby with the U. K. Government to have Confederation also placed on the ballot. They collected nearly fifty thousand signatures and asked the Governor Gordon MacDonald to send these to the British government, to demonstrate the real wishes of the people. MacDonald was glad to do this, as you will see later. The lobby was successful and on March 2, 1948, it was announced that in three months a referendum would be held, with the three choices on the paper. For the next three months a vigorous campaign was fought throughout the country. Peter Cashin formed "The Responsible Government League" "and published a weekly newspaper called *The Independent.* Smallwood formed "The Newfoundland Confederate Association" and put out a weekly entitled *The*

Frank Kennedy opens the door for Premier Smallwood.

Confederate. This latter newspaper was printed by The *Daily News*, and I remember Smallwood was very insistent on the paper coming out on the same day each week.

Joey Gives Everyone Fifty Dollars

One week, on the day before publication, it was thought the issue might be late. Smallwood visited the *Daily News* and got the names of all the printers, etc. who were working on the paper. He went personally to each employee and offered them fifty dollars each, if they would come back to work for a couple of hours after supper to finish the job. He came up to the photo-engraving department and handed John O'Brien and myself fifty dollars each to finish some engravings of photos he needed. Of course, we all came back to work that night, regardless of political affiliation, and The *Daily News* paid us overtime as well (which was charged to *The Confederate*; talk about double dipping!).

When the votes were counted on June 3, Responsible Government was the winner with 69,400. Confederation with Canada came a close second at 64,066, and Commission Government a poor third with 22,311. Had any party received 77,889 votes, this would have been a majority, but this did not happen, so a second referendum was called for July 22, 1948, with Commission Government left off the ballot. This time the Confederates won with a slim six-percent majority of the votes: Confederation, 78,323, Responsible Government, 71,334. The government of Canada accepted that as adequate approval by the people of Newfoundland, and immediately invited a delegation to Ottawa to negotiate the final terms of union. These delegates were Gordon Bradley, Albert Walsh, Ches. Crosbie, Phillip Grouchy, Joseph Smallwood, John B. McEvoy and Gordon Winter. The terms were signed on December 11, 1948, but Ches Crosbie didn't think Newfoundland was getting a fair deal and refused to sign. Two months later the Terms were accepted by the Canadian parliament, and it was announced that Newfoundland would become Canada's tenth province one minute before midnight on March 31, 1949. Smallwood did not want his greatest aim in life to be fulfilled on April Fool's Day, although fiscal years for Canadian governments normally begin on April 1.

I mentioned earlier that Governor Gordon MacDonald was glad to send the nearly fifty thousand signatures to Britain. Here's the reason for his delight: he was actually sent out from England in 1946 to discreetly make sure that Newfoundland entered Confederation. That fact was not widely known at the time, and I'm sure many Newfoundlanders are still not aware of it. The Progressive Conservatives knew about it, and in 1997, Newfoundland historian Dr. John Fitzgerald was in England and spoke with the daughter of the late Gordon MacDonald. She would not deny that this was her father's mandate, nor would she confirm it. She simply said that her father was in favor of Newfoundland joining Canada.

The Tribute

MacDonald's term as the last Governor of Newfoundland (as a country) ended on March 31, 1949. On Tuesday, March 8, there appeared on the editorial page of the *Evening Telegram* what seemed to be a great tribute to Governor MacDonald, noting the countless thousands who were praying for his safe return to England, and mentioning the love "...we, the people, have for him." It was a masterpiece of deception, however, as it turned out to be an acronym, and the first letter of each line spelled "The Bastard," This is the tribute:

The prayer of countless thousands sent
Heavenward to speed thy safe return,
Ennobled, as thou art, with duty well performed.
Bringing peace, security and joy
Among the peoples of this New Found Land,
So saddened and depressed until your presence
Taught us all discern, and helped decide what's best for
All on whom fortune had not smiled.
Remember, if you will, the kindness and the love,
Devotion and the rest, that we the people have for thee.

Farewell

The *Evening Telegram* editors, of course, would never have published it had they realized what it really was, and very shortly after the paper hit the streets the embarrassed publishers sent their delivery vans around St. John's to retrieve all the unsold copies. The piece was the work of prominent P. C. supporters Grace Sparkes, Chief Justice Robert Furlong, and prominent lawyer and Q. C. Jack Higgins. The latter two gentlemen are now deceased. The authorship remained a secret for decades except to a select few, and I have, in fact, never seen their names published. Their anonymous letter to the *Telegram* read, "Dear Mr. Editor, would you publish the attached farewell to His Excellency, Sir Gordon MacDonald, K. C. M.G."

Grace Sparkes, circa 1963.
Photo by John O'Brien

In January 1999, I spoke with my friend Grace Sparkes, now Dr. Sparkes, and asked for her permission to use her name as one of the authors. Her reply, "Well, I'll be drawn and quartered and my clothes burned, but go ahead. What odds! I'm ninety now, and I don't care." Thanks, Gracie! She added that Ed Roberts tried for years to find out who the authors were, and to the best of her knowledge, he never did find out. In his book *No Holds Barred*, John Crosbie says not only did many Newfoundlanders dislike MacDonald for his strong confederate leanings, but also because he was opposed to drinking and card-playing. Crosbie prints the "poetic farewell" and attributes it to "Newfoundlanders' wicked sense of humor." Crosbie does not say who wrote it, so he probably didn't know either. When MacDonald returned to England, he was rewarded for his efforts. He was made a peer of England, and received the title of baron. This title could also be passed on to his descendants. He was sixty years of age at that time and lived another seventeen years, passing away on January 20, 1966.

April 1, 1949

On this first full day of Confederation, special ceremonies took place in Government House in St. John's, in front of more than two dozen members from the media, both local and foreign. Don Jamieson, then a reporter, covered for the *Sunday Herald*, Mark Ronayne and Albert Young for the *Evening Telegram*, Ed Quigley for the *Gerald S. Doyle News Bulletin* on radio, and Jack White and myself for the *Daily News*, as well as Russ Roberts and Gordon Barron. Many dignitaries were present as the first lieutenant governor of the new province, Sir Albert Walsh, was sworn in by Chief Justice Sir Edward Emerson. Walsh invited Smallwood to form an interim administration of the government, until a general election could be held. Joey had his prospective cabinet ministers all ready, and they were sworn in as well.

Smallwood, always one to seize opportunities, took advantage of the large press gathering and held his first press conference right there in Government House. Smallwood wanted to assure the people of Newfoundland that the old age pensions and baby bonuses would be delivered even before the elections took place. During his campaign for Confederation, he had repeatedly emphasized these were two of the great blessings of joining Canada. He also promised that the election would be held before the hundreds of fishermen left the island for the summer Labrador fishery. Asked if he would become leader of any political party, he said he had no comment at this time, but hoped to become the first elected premier of Newfoundland.

In less than two months, on May 27, a general election was held. Smallwood had become leader of the newly constituted Newfoundland Liberal Party. Peter Cashin ran as an independent, and Harry Mews led the Progressive Conservatives. Mews and convention member Michael Harrington ran in St. John's West and both were defeated by the Liberals Al Vardy and James Spratt. Smallwood ran in Bonavista North and severely beat his opponent, P. C. Kitchener Prichett, by 3560 votes out of a total of 4268. For the Liberals it was a landslide victory. The results were twenty-two seats for them and only five for the P.C.s. The election for the one seat for Labrador was delayed because of the weather, and was held in July, when Harold Horwood picked up another seat for the Liberals. Since the P. Cs. were now without an elected leader, they persuaded Cashin, who had been elected an independent, to join them and become their new leader. The standing in the House was now Liberals twenty-three and Progressive Conservatives six. The Liberals would remain in power for twenty-three years, through five more elections. Their biggest term being September 1966 to September 1971, when they held thirty-nine seats, with the P. C.s holding three. The election of March 24, 1972, however, was a stunning upset, with the P. C. s winning thirty-three seats and the Liberals down to nine.

Smallwood's First Press Conference After Confederation

Smallwood held the conference in Government House, as soon as he was sworn in as leader of the interim government. Left to right in front are Ed Quigley, for the *Gerald S. Doyle News* on radio; Don Jamieson, then a reporter for the *Sunday Herald*, and Jack White for *The Daily News*. Behind Quigley is Alex Thompson for the *Evening Telegram*. Smallwood is at center. Top to bottom are Joe MacSween, the *Canadian Press*, Albert Young, *The Evening Telegram* and Gordon Barron, *The Daily News*. At center, top, is myself, Frank Kennedy.

Other Local News Items for the Year 1949

Jan. 9	R. C. A. F. Rec. Hall at Goose Bay Airport destroyed by fire. $250,000 damage.
Jan. 16	Air Mail service to Great Northern Peninsula inaugurated.
Jan. 19	Dr. Nigel Rusted appointed Medical Supervisor at Grace Hospital.
Jan. 31	Fire at Lewisporte destroys two hotels and doctors residence.
Feb. 1	Fire destroys Snow's Hotel in Millertown.
Mar. 6	Governor MacDonald and family leave for England.
Mar. 12	Railway bridge at South West River, Port Blanford, carried away in washout.
Mar. 15	Noon-day gun on Signal Hill fires for last time. Said to be too expensive.
Mar. 31	*M. V. Terra Nova*'s first arrival from the ice fields.

	Honorable F. Gordon Bradley, K. C., appointed first Newfoundland minister in Canadian cabinet.
Apr. 7	Serious food shortage reported at St. Mary's River, Labrador.
Apr. 9	Supplies of food dropped by plane to inhabitants of St. Mary's River. Bandit holds up Bank of Montreal in Curling. Gets away.
Apr. 28	St. Lawrence miners go on strike.
May 11	Harbour Grace North West Fish Ltd. workers go on strike.
June 6	Enlistment of Newfoundlanders into Canadian Armed Forces begins.
June 7	W. J. Browne resigns as judge. Will enter Federal politics.
June 8	Newfoundland's first Provincial government officially sworn in.
June 13	W. J. Browne demands arrest of J. R. Smallwood on grounds of intimidating voters of Ferryland.
June 26	Plane crash at Harmon Field, injures three.
June 28	Magistrate O'Neill sets July 7 as date for Smallwood trial.
July 6	No bus service in St. John's as drivers and mechanics of Golden Arrow Bus Co. go on strike.
July 7	Smallwood case postponed.
July 13	Paving of Water Street begins.
July 21	City buses roll again as two-week strike ends

Aug. 10	Severe storm hits Labrador in middle of summer fishery. One vessel lost and severe damage caused to fishing gear.
Aug. 11	Bill to raise Memorial College to status of university, gets second reading in House.
Aug. 17	Sir Leonard Outerbridge appointed Lieutenant Governor of Newfoundland, to succeed Sir Albert Walsh, who will become Chief Justice.
Aug. 18	Dr. Florence O'Neill appointed acting Director of Adult Education. Corner Brook Co-op store destroyed in $300,000 fire.
Sept. 18	*M. S. Bargfield* wrecked on Cape St. Mary's. All crew saved. United States Base Command lays off six hundred civilians in Newfoundland.
Sept..20	Baxter Wareham and Elsworth Taylor drown in Gander Lake.
Oct. 9	Bowaters sets new daily production record. 1010 tons of paper in twenty-four hours.
Oct. 31	Justice Winter rules Smallwood entitled to jury trial.
Nov. 16	Small U. S. plane crashes off Flat Rock. Pilot rescued by fishermen.
Dec. 16	Telephone circuit opened, St. John's to Port-aux-Basques.
Dec. 20	*M. V. Keltic* lost off Cape St. Mary's. Crew saved.

Stadium Cornerstone Laid by Barbara Ann Scott

On St. John's Day, June 24, 1950, the cornerstone of the new stadium in the city was laid by Canadian and World Champion olympic figure skater, Barbara Ann Scott. Thousands turned out for the gala event held near the head of Quidi Vidi Lake, and the visiting band of the Prince Edward Island Highlanders in their red uniforms added color and lively music to the celebration of the start of the much needed facility. The celebrity had been flown to St. John's the previous day, compliments of the Department of Transport. With a shiny silver trowel in hand, she said to the excited audience, "I can't tell you how thrilled I am to lay the cornerstone of your new stadium." Miss Scott had been introduced by R. B. Herder of the St. John's Stadium Company. Other dignitaries present included the Lieutenant Governor, Sir Leonard Outerbridge; Premier J. R.

Barbara Ann Scott lays cornerstone for new Stadium, June 24, 1950.

The St. John's Memorial Stadium. Cornerstone laid in 1950.

Smallwood; Lions Club President Doug Pinsent; President of the Stadium Company, P. E. Outerbridge; Mayor H. G. R. Mews and former mayor Andy Carnell. Earlier, Mayor Mews paid tribute to Carnell and the previous city council for donating, free of charge, the land on which the stadium would be built. He gave full credit to the St. John's Lions Club for launching a campaign to get the building started. Thanks to their efforts, he said, nearly all workers in St. John's, (including myself) had pledged one percent of their wages to the stadium fund. We were called "One Percenters." The building would be known as the St. John's Memorial Stadium, in memory of those who gave their lives in two world wars. Mews presented the deed to the property to Outerbridge, and assured him that the present council would charge no city taxes on the new stadium. This statement was endorsed by a great round of applause from the audience. Outerbridge thanked the mayor, and also thanked the *Daily News*, the *Evening Telegram*, and radio station *VOCM* for all their free advertising. Then he introduced Premier Smallwood.

Miss Scott meets the local press at the reception in her honor at Government House.

Smallwood's main interest in having this large building was to encourage farmers, fishermen and factory workers to participate in a once-a-year gigantic fair, where great prizes would be given for the best products. He said the provincial government was giving an interest-free loan of $1 million provided that one day a year would be set aside for a giant crafts, agricultural, and fisheries fair, and he said this loan was only a start. After three years, the Federal Government would donate $10,000 per year for ten years, provided the one-day fair was held, with prizes worth at least $6000 each year. Then, looking towards Barbara Ann Scott, he declared, "This is on behalf of all Newfoundland men over the age of twelve," and then he planted a kiss on her cheek!

The next speaker, ex-Mayor Andy Carnell, said the development of a stadium at the head on Quidi Vidi Lake had long been dear to his heart. After a short speech, he looked at Miss Scott and said, "Joey is not going to steal my tune!" And with that, he too kissed the beautiful star on the cheek, to uproarious applause. Then with the silver trowel, Miss Scott spread fresh mortar on the corner stone, to officially set it in place. Barbara Ann wished good luck to the stadium, and congratulated the Lions Club for their fine work. Then she unveiled a large painting of the completed building, and told the audience that she hoped she could come back and skate there when the stadium was opened. The Lions Club presented her with a magnificent fur wrap, which she immediately put on and was obviously thrilled. Confederation had taken place only the previous year, and Miss Scott welcomed the new Province on behalf of all Canadians. Then she went into the crowd and was swarmed by autograph seekers, scores of whom she obliged. Later that day we were invited to Government House to cover a reception for Miss Scott, hosted by Sir Leonard and Mrs. Outerbridge. That night, there was a big street dance on Water Street, and the highlight of that affair was when Miss Scott arrived, riding in the back of an open convertible. Hundreds of fans gathered around, and the car barely crawled along the street before being forced to stop. Once again the autograph seekers crowded in, and once again she obliged. It was half an hour before the car could at last move on, amidst the cheering and waving of the happy people who continued celebrating and dancing into the late hours of the night.

The Sinking of the *S.S. Eagle*

"She was a good ship."
—William Dormandy, retired crew member.

On July 23, 1950, the old wooden sealing ship *S. S. Eagle* sailed through the St. John's Narrows for the last time. Having outlived her usefulness, the vessel was towed to the Cordelia Deeps, a few miles north-east of the harbour, and sent to the bottom in 600 feet of water. The ship was given a great send-off, being escorted by more than twenty vessels of various sizes including the *Eastern Explorer*, from which reporter Russ Roberts and myself covered the story for the *Daily News*.

The *S.S. Eagle* sails through the narrows for the last time on July 23, 1950. In forty-four years of service the ship had brought in nearly one and a half million dollars worth of seal pelts. *Photo by Ted Caines Courtesy of Marilyn Burt*

It was a fine summer Sunday afternoon, and thousands lined the waterfront, the Battery, Signal Hill and the south side, as the tug *Glemont*, Captain Smith in charge, gently eased the old steamer away from Bowring's wharf on the south side of the harbour, with two tow lines in place. On board was a skeleton crew, with Captain George Anstey acting as pilot. As the *Eagle* passed Chain Rock with all signal flags flying, ships' sirens and whistles sounded a final farewell, and applause and cheering could be heard coming from the Battery and Signal Hill.

The trip to the Deeps, just off Sugar Loaf, took two hours. About halfway along, one of the tow-lines broke. Another tug, *M. V. Ice Hunter*, was standing by, but was not needed as the other hawser held. Having reached the pre-planned location, the tug "hove to" and dropped the remaining tow-line. On board the old sealer, the sea-cocks were opened, and the last man to leave the ship was Mr. James Grieve, director of Bowring Brothers, the own-

Signal flags still flying, the *S. S. Eagle* begins it's final trip—600 feet to the bottom of the ocean. *Photo by Ted Caines Courtesy Marilyn Burt.*

The deck of the *S. S. Eagle*, that had seen seven hundred thousand seal pelts come aboard, slips gently beneath the waves. *Photo by Ted Caines Courtesy Marilyn Burt.*

ers. Mr. Grieve stood alone on the deck that had seen nearly seven hundred thousand seals come aboard, looked around a final time, and descended the rope ladder to the waiting pilot boat. It took the vessel two hours to go down, and as the flotilla circled, artificial red smoke rose from the deck giving the illusion the ship was on fire. Mr. W. Dormandy was a crew member on the *Eagle* forty-seven years earlier when she first came to Newfoundland, having been built in Norway in 1902. He was with us on the Explorer, and as the proud ship slipped beneath the waves, with tears in his eyes, Mr. Dormandy waved farewell and declared, "She was a good ship." Mr. Hubert Warfield was also with us; he had made several trips aboard the *Eagle*, and watched in silence as the vessel disappeared.

The steam-ship *Eagle*, a coal burner, displaced just under five hundred tons, was 176 feet long, with a beam of 29 feet, and had gone "to the ice" for forty-four years, bringing back nearly $1.5 million worth of seals. The best year was 1916, when the catch was 33,400, valued at $74,000. When I was asked to photograph the sinking, not knowing how bad a sailor I am, I was glad to go along. However, I never dreamed the trip would take six hours, and after two hours, I was leaning over the rail quite a bit. Someone kindly suggested I should lie on a bunk in the cabin, and this I did, and was able to keep an eye on proceedings through a porthole. Nevertheless, every fifteen or twenty minutes, I had to make a run for the railing, and maybe take a picture while I was up. Once, as I lay there in misery, a crew member offered me some soda crackers. I remember saying, "No, thank you, just throw them over the side; that will save me a trip."

Other Local News Items for the Year 1950

Jan. 2	Mayor H. G. R. Mews and new city council officially take over the running of St. John's.
Jan. 18	E. P. A. plane crashes at LaScie.

Jan. 22	Rev. Patrick J. Skinner appointed Titular Bishop of St. John's.
Feb. 16	St. John's Harbour closed as Arctic ice blocks Narrows.
Feb. 21	St. John's Harbour open again as ice moves off.
Mar. 27	*M. V. Algerine* arrives in St. John's with 24,000 pelts.
Mar. 28	Premier announces new discoveries of lead, zinc and copper at Buchans.
Apr. I	Arctic Sealer *Captain Hill* arrives St. John's with 18,300 pelts.
Apr. 3	First floating fish filleting factory ship, *S. S. Fairfree* from Scotland, operating on Grand Banks.
Apr. 4	*S. S. Terra Nova* arrives from icefields with 11,000 seals.
Apr. 8	Portuguese fishing fleet arrives in St. John's for summer fishing season. Twenty-five hundred men.
Apr. 14	Government announced today that Family Allowance payments for first year of Confederation amounted to $10 million.
Apr. 25	*S. S. Newfoundland* arrives in St. John's with 17,000 pelts.
Apr. 26	Budget presented in House of Assembly. Estimated expenditure $38 million. Revenue $26. 5 million.
May 5	Salt Codfish Association deeply concerned large surplus of fish unsold.

May 12	Premier Smallwood honored by Blackfoot Indians in Alberta.
May 15	Eastern Provincial Airways fined for landing plane on Windsor Lake, city's water supply.
May 24	Alfred Valdmanis appointed advisor to Economic Development.
June 12	Schooner *Flora Nicholson* total loss at Wesleyville.
June 24	Barbara Ann Scott lays cornerstone new stadium in St. John's.
June 30	Famous singer, Gracie Fields, arrives in St. John's.
July 26	New boathouse at Quidi Vidi Lake officially opened.
July 31	R.C.M.P. absorbs the Newfoundland Ranger Force.
Aug. 25	Blueberries sell at $1.00 per gallon.
Sep. 18	Water Street department store, James Baird Ltd, closes after nearly one hundred years in business.
Sep. 20	Ferd Hayward wins twenty mile walk in time of 3 Hrs. 2 Min. 55 Sec.
Sep. 23	Roman Catholic archbishop of St. John's, Most Rev. Edward Patrick Roache passes away.
Sep. 28	Thousands attend funeral of late Archbishop.
Oct. 26	Walter Sweeney sentenced to twenty years for manslaughter.
Nov. 4	Ethel Tucker found murdered in her home at St. Phillip's.

Nov. 9	100,000 lbs. flounder dumped for lack of filleters.
Nov. 13	Three men charged with the murder of Ethel Tucker
Dec. 21	Bowring Brothers Limited donates $10,000 to stadium fund

The Royal Visit, November 11, 1951

SCOTLAND YARD WARNING! -
"We won't photograph Her Royal Highness while she's eating, will we?"

In 1951, Queen Elizabeth, who was then princess and heir to the throne, visited Newfoundland for the first time. It was the last stop of a five-week, cross-Canada tour, and Her Royal Highness and husband Prince Philip, the duke of Edinburgh, stayed in St. John's two days. Arriving on Sunday morning November 11, on board the Canadian Cruiser *H. M. C. S. Ontario*, the warship docked at the Furness Withy Pier on Water Street east, in the presence of Guards of Honor from the Canadian Army, Navy, and Air Force. Also on hand were the Lieutenant Governor, Sir Leonard Outerbridge; Premier Smallwood; Mayor Mews, and other dignitaries, as well as the press. The public were not permitted on the premises, but anxiously lined the pre-announced route of the royal procession. As the ship gently touched the pier, with the crew standing at attention along the rails, one of the sailors could be seen hurriedly swabbing the deck at the entrance to the gangplank with mop and bucket. He quickly disappeared and the princess came on deck, followed by the duke. On this chilly November morning, she looked comfortable and lovely in her dark mink coat, as she shook hands with the Navy crew and bade them goodbye. Walking down the gangplank, she turned to the men and waved, and this gesture was acknowledged by a great round of applause and spontaneous cheering from the sailors.

On shore, the royal couple were welcomed by the Lieutenant Governor, who introduced the premier, the mayor and the cabinet ministers. After reviewing the honor guards from the armed forces, the couple were escorted to a plastic-domed Cadillac, which took them a few hundred yards west on Water Street to the War Memorial. Along the way, thousands of people on the sidewalks applauded and cheered, and hundreds of children waved their colorful flags. This was Armistice Day, of course, and it was now close to eleven o'clock, the traditional time at which Memorial services were held every year, to remember the war that ended on the eleventh hour of the eleventh day of the eleventh month. As usual, hundreds of war veterans and members of the Armed Forces were lined up, and thousands of spectators were waiting to witness the wreath-laying ceremony. Today was extra special: the princess had chosen Newfoundland, of all places in Canada, to participate in the annual memorial service. The veterans particularly were aware of this, and openly talked about how special it made them feel.

When the Royal car arrived at the cenotaph, there was great excitement. Cheering and wild applause greeted the visitors, and it was obvious the soldiers present had great difficulty restraining themselves; but in true military style, they remained standing at attention, stone-faced and looking straight ahead, until the order, "At ease!" was given. A short ceremony followed, during which the royal couple laid a large wreath which bore the following inscription:

> In Memory of the Glorious Dead
> Elizabeth and Philip
> Clarence House
> St. James's Court

The princess and duke shook hands with many of the war veterans, including one gentleman with a white cane. Afterwards, *News* reporter Marg Grouchy spoke with him. His name was

Charles Davey. He had lost one eye in battle in France in 1917, and the other in Belgium the following year. He said he often thought how unlucky he was to lose both eyes, but today he had the "thrill of a lifetime." The duke had touched his hand and asked his name. Then he introduced him to the princess, and he said he recognized her pretty feminine voice as she spoke to him, and as he timidly put out his hand, the princess gave him a warm handshake. He said he knew then that the sacrifice was not in vain. It was all worth while! As the princess and duke left the monument, the crowd broke through the police lines to get a closer look, but at no time was the royal couple's safety threatened. Driving up Water Street, the procession passed through a huge green spruce-bough archway which spanned the width of the street, then on to the Anglican Cathedral for a special one-hour service. At the same time a memorial mass was being celebrated at the Roman Catholic Cathedral (now the Basilica), just up the road, and there a message was read from Archbishop Skinner, expressing to their royal highnesses, the loyalty and affection of the Catholic people of the archdiocese of St. John's. Next stop for the royal couple was Government House for just fifteen minutes, then off to the Old Colony Club on Portugal Cove Road for the formal Newfoundland government luncheon. It was a busy day for the princess!

It had been decided earlier by the authorities that as space was limited, only one local press photographer and one local reporter would be allowed at the luncheon, and that the two newspapers should pool their photos. There was no television in Newfoundland in those days. I was honored to be selected to cover this prestigious affair for both papers, and our reporter Ann Perlin would write the story. The ballroom was tastefully decorated, and the white linen tablecloths formed appropriate backgrounds for the one thousand red roses and dozens of yellow and bronze chrysanthemums. There were 150 invited guests, and the menu listed such local delicacies as creamed codfish, Newfoundland venison and Labrador Ice Cream with blueberry syrup. I was given no previous instructions regarding protocol, as we always were in later years for such events, and so during the meal, I got up from the press table with my big camera and approached the head table. Out of nowhere, a Scotland Yard special officer appeared and intercepted me, and with a perfect British accent whispered into my ear, "We won't photograph Her Royal Highness while she's eating, will we?" And with perfect townie accent, I replied, "Of course not!" I sheepishly returned to the press table, sat down and finished my meal, as Her Royal Highness finished hers, with no fear of being photographed while eating.

Following the gourmet lunch, the Lieutenant Governor Sir Leonard Outerbridge proposed a toast to His Majesty The King, after which Premier Smallwood did the same for Her Royal Highness. In a very eloquent (although uncharacteristically short) speech, Smallwood once more extended a warm welcome to the royal couple and stated how honored we were to have them visit

Premier Smallwood presents princess Elizabeth with a Newfoundland Otter fur cape during formal luncheon at Old Colony Club in November, 1951. Daily News *Photo by Frank Kennedy*

us. All present stood and drank that toast and Smallwood then presented her with a handsome Newfoundland otter-fur cape, on behalf of the people of the province. The duke was given an envelope knife with an exquisitely carved ivory handle. The princess was obviously delighted, and before addressing the gathering, passed the cape along to her lady-in-waiting. Then she proceeded to thank the premier for his kindness. She said, "I want to thank you very much indeed, for the words in which you have proposed the toast, and the way in which you have honored it. We are very grateful for the gifts and shall value them, because they will always make us think of our first visit to this province, which has such close ties to Britain." She said she would like to see Newfoundland in the summer, not that there is anything wrong with November; "...but the strongest force which will draw us back here, is the warmth of the welcome we have received this morning from your fine people. We shall never forget it. We wish we could have stayed to see more of your province, but that must wait for another time, which, we hope, will be not too far distant." When the princess sat down after extended applause, she turned and spoke to Smallwood, who was seated at her side. He nodded, stood up and walked to the lady-in-waiting, and brought back the cape. The princess wished to have a closer look. She showed it to the duke, and they could be seen feeling the soft, luxurious fur. One of the CBC radio reporters, seated at our table, told us he had followed the tour right across Canada, and had watched the princess receive numerous gifts along the way. He said he had never seen such a reaction to any of the other presents. She was obviously very thrilled with this one.

Later, Smallwood told us he was very impressed with the princess. He said she has a great sense of humor, and can really tell a joke, as well as enjoy listening to one. When asked for more details, he observed, "Of course, it wouldn't be fair to tell what the jokes were about, without her permission. "Smallwood was surprised at her knowledge of Newfoundland. She asked about the people, and what they did for a living, besides the fishery. He mentioned that we have the biggest paper mill in the world." Oh, yes," she said, "Bowaters, I know about that; it's in Corner Brook."

When he mentioned another large paper mill in Grand Falls, she said, "Yes, that's the large industry Lord Beaverbrook started." (A. N.D. Company). The premier mentioned the Bell Island mines, which were in full production at that time, and she said she'd been hearing for years about the famous mines that run miles out under the sea. Smallwood told us he was privileged to talk with such a charming member of the royal family. He was delighted to discover that the future queen is so interested in Newfoundland and its people.

Leaving the Old Colony Club, the royal motorcade made a tour of the city, going as far west as Road de Luxe, much to the delight of thousands of people who again lined the route. Many had come a considerable distance to see the popular Princess. In the meantime, at Government House, three hundred people had gathered to await the arrival which occurred at 4:00 p. m. Another reception followed, as which all present were introduced to their royal highnesses. That concluded the official functions for the day, and the royal party were guests of Sir Leonard and Mrs. Outerbridge for the night. Monday being the final day of the Royal visit to Canada, the princess broadcasted a farewell message to the country which was carried across the dominion on the CBC radio network. The broadcast was made from "The Morning Room" at Government House. This room had been newly decorated for the occasion, and the *Daily News* described it as, "Now the gayest room in Government House, with its new color scheme of bright autumn hues of greens, bronze and chartreuse, in the chintz slipcovers and drapes."

After the broadcast, another short tour of the east end of the city followed, and ended at the Fieldian Grounds on Portugal Cove Road for a short farewell ceremony. On the field, no less than thirteen bands waited to be heard by the royal couple, including the well known Mount Cashel Band and various cadet bands. As the motorcade arrived, the R.C.A.F. band struck up The National Anthem. The Princess inspected troops of the Royal Newfoundland Regiment, and was presented with a beautiful morocco-bound photo album containing thirty Newfoundland scenes. This presentation was made by Mrs. J. Boyd Baird, on behalf of the thirty thousand Newfoundland members of the Imperial Daughters of the British Empire. In thanking Mrs. Baird, the princess said these pictures would frequently remind her of her visit, and the many friendships she made while here in Newfoundland. To the strains of "We'll Rant and We'll Roar Like True Newfoundlanders," the royal couple drove away from their last official function of the five-week tour of Canada. At Portugal Cove, the departure point, the weather was desperate: cold, raining, windy and stormy. Nevertheless, thousands waited to bid farewell to the royal visitors. On the old wooden pier, the Church Lads Brigade (CLB) band stood, drenched in the rain. On one side the small ferry *Maneco* was moored. This would take the royal party up Conception Bay to the waiting *Empress of Scotland*. On the other side, the ferry *Kippewa* was tied up, with hundreds of children from Bell Island lining the rails. A dozen fishing boats strained at their anchors, as waves washed over the smaller one. When the Cadillac drove out on the wharf, the CLB band began playing the national anthem as the duke stepped from the car. Just then a large wave struck the *Kippewa*, causing it to bump the pier with a severe jolt. The royal car, with the princess still sitting in the rear seat, shook vigorously, and she was obviously quite frightened. The duke reassured her, and as she alighted, placed a rain cape over her shoulders. He was bare headed. Cabinet ministers lining the wharf had difficulty keeping their top hats in place, as the Princess again shook hands before going on board the ferry. There, some fishermen presented a small wooden box of salt fish, as the band played, "The Squid Jiggin' Grounds." As the boat moved away, "Auld Lang Syne" could be heard above the howling of the wind, as the princess and duke waved farewell.

The lieutenant governor and the premier expressed concern at the fierce storm, but some Portugal Cove fishermen told them not to worry. The skilled skipper had taken the *Maneco* to Bell Island in worse seas than this, they said. A few hundred feet out, the boat seemed to be headed for rocks on the south side of the cove, and a cry of distress was heard coming from the shore, but the Captain quickly reversed the engine, and the crisis was averted. A flotilla of fishing boats attempted to escort the *Maneco*

A wave washes over the ferry *Maneco*, as it leaves Portugal Cove, with the royal couple on board in 1951. Daily News *Photo by Frank Kennedy. Courtesy Provincial Reference Library.*

to the waiting ocean liner, but the seas were too heavy, and one after the other, they had to turn back. Later that day, Sir Leonard received a telegram from the captain of the *Empress*, saying that the royal party had gotten safely on board, and were now happily on their way home to England. Eight years later, in June 1959, Elizabeth did return to Newfoundland, this time as queen, having been crowned in 1953. As she had hoped, she was able to see more of the province, visiting not only St. John's but the west coast as well, including Corner Brook and Deer Lake. Once again she expressed delight at the lovely Newfoundland scenery.

Other Local News Events for the Year 1951

Jan. 1	Fishery Products dragger, *St. Richard's* sinks on the Grand Banks, one man dead.
Jan. 5	Premier Smallwood opens new hospital at Corner Brook.

Jan. 9	Honorable J.J. Spratt announced government would pass act elimi--nating half hour time difference in Newfoundland.
Jan. 11	Grand Jury brings in true bill against H. Hiscock, M. Evans and Vic Rumsey for murder of Ethel Tucker of St. Phillip's.
Jan. 22	H.W. Sheppard & Sons saw mill at Spaniard's Bay destroyed in $50,000 fire.
Jan. 24	Three new senators appointed: Herman Quintan, Cal Pratt, Michael Basha.
Jan. 25	Bell Island Mines awarded million ton iron ore contract with Great Britain.
Jan. 29	Tucker Murder trial begins, three men charged.
Jan. 30	Most Rev. P. J. Skinner appointed Archbishop of St. John's
	United Church, Bishop's Falls destroyed by fire.
Feb. 3	United Nations Children's Emergency Fund purchased five hundred tons Newfoundland salt codfish.
Feb. 8	Three men convicted of manslaughter in death of Ethel Tucker of St. Phillip's.
Feb. 22	Premier Smallwood announces government to contribute $20,000 to help fishermen organize.
Mar. 6	Federal government refused request of provinces to collect more than 3% sales tax.
Mar. 15	Baby born to Mrs. Everett Cox of St. Alban's, on board R. C. A. F. plane 2000 feet above Newfoundland.

Mar. 22	Sealer *Lady MacDonald* crushed by ice off Cape Norman and sinks. *M.V.Linda May* rescues crew.
Mar. 31	*M. V. Arctic Sealer*, first arrival this year from the ice fields, brings in 35,500 pelts.
Apr. 8	Two sealing ships arrive from the ice fields; *M. V. Exploits* and *Ice Hunter*.
Apr. 12	Landslide at Gambo ties up railway.
Apr. 20	Three ships sail for second trip to the ice: *Algerina, Ice Hunter* and *Exploits*.
Apr. 25	Sealer *M. V. Trepassey* arrives from the ice fields.
Apr. 29	Sealer *M. V. Newfoundland* arrives from the ice fields.
May 3	*M. V. Terra Nova* arrives from the ice fields.
May 4	*M. V. Glenwood* arrives from the ice fields.
May 18	His Grace Archbishop Skinner receives the pallium from the Pope at Vatican City.
May 22	Trade Printers premises badly damaged by fire.
May 24	Hottest May 24 in local history, eighty-two degrees in the sun.
May 26	First Newfoundland casualty in Korean war. Private Leo J. Lawlor of St. John's, killed in action.
May 30	Gladys Freeman of Long Pond, Manuels, first woman to enlist in R. C. A. F.
June 6	Last arrival from the ice fields, *M. V. Placentia*," brings home the key."

July 10	Premier Smallwood and group of Swiss industrialists sign contract for machine manufacturing plant in Newfoundland.
Aug. 1	Annual regatta cut short as bad weather sets in.
Aug. 6	John Bird of Cartwright, Labrador, charged with murder of his wife.
Aug. 9	Premier Smallwood announces four million dollar textile plant to be built near St. John's.
Aug. 14	Explosion on board Spanish trawler at Imperial Oil premises or Southside kills Andres Villar, forty year old crewman.
Aug. 15	Explosion on board long liner, *Miss Osboone* at Bonavista, injures three men.
Aug. 21	Premier Smallwood and Attorney General Les Curtis, leave to visit industrial cities in Europe.
	DOSCO lays off eighteen hundred workers on Bell Island because of unauthorized strike.
Aug. 29	Miners return to work in Bell Island Mines after one week layoff.
Sept. 20	Seven men, including three Newfoundlanders, killed as Buchans Mining Company plane crashes in central Newfoundland.
	Sir Eric Bowater announces $ 10 million expansion to Corner Brook paper mill.
Sept. 24	Smallwood announces the new machine plant will be located at Octagon Pond.

Oct. 10	New local radio station CJON officially opened.
Oct. 27	U. S. airman swept off cliff at Quidi Vidi Village by huge wave and drowned.
Nov. 1	Population of Newfoundland announced as 357,762.
Nov. 19	Premier Smallwood officially opens Cement Plant at Corner Brook.
Dec. 2	Ayre & Sons Ltd. opens new supermarket , on the corner of Parade Street & Harvey Road.
Dec. 18	A. E. Hickman's warehouse in Corner Brook destroyed by fire. $250,000 damage.
Dec. 19	Ninety-mile-an-hour winds and giant waves force six hundred residents from their homes in Stephenville. Heavy damage in Labrador.

The Family Rosary Crusade, 1952.

"The Family That Prays Together, Stays Together. "
—Father Patrick Peyton, CSC

It was one of the largest gatherings in Newfoundland, except for the annual regatta, when on Sunday, September 14, 1952, fifteen thousand people of various denominations waited for hours in the pouring rain to see and hear world-renowned Jesuit priest, Father Patrick Peyton, at St. Pat's Ball Park in St. John's. It was the culmination of a crusade that started a month earlier in Newfoundland, to urge Christian families to recite the rosary every day. A planned parade through the city, from St. Clare's Hospital to the Ball Park, was canceled because of the weather, but the service would go ahead at 4:00 p. m. People started arriving with their umbrellas as early as two o'clock, and soon the five thousand seats were filled, but ten thousand more came and remained standing in front of a seventy-foot long platform on which stood a twenty-five foot high altar. This altar was tastefully decorated with the blue and white theme, the recognized colors of the Blessed Virgin. On either side were gold crosses in wooden panels, and the platform was outlined with thousands of flowers. Overhead the slogan, "The Family That Prays Together Stays Together," was surmounted by a huge rosary in lights.

Amongst the crowd on the field were representatives of various parishes, and the banners they proudly displayed included Conception Bay, Placentia, St. Mary's, Southern Shore and the Burin Peninsula. Rev. Fr. G. J. Murphy began the service by reciting the rosary, which was responded to by thousands of voices. Then the Director of the Family Rosary Crusade, Fr. John B. Kent, introduced Father Peyton. Father Kent traced the priest's life back to his early boyhood in Ireland. There, in a modest home, the love of the "Blessed Lady" was born in his young heart. The lesson of the importance of family prayer was so deeply imprinted on his mind that he dedicated his adult life to spreading love for the Mother of God throughout the world, and devoted his efforts to establishing family prayer in every Christian home. Father Kent said that "... today we are privileged to hear his appeal and hear him prove his famous slogan. The many thousands who have come to hear him are a tribute to the spirit of religion so characteristic of the people of our beloved Newfoundland. "Father Peyton, obviously very impressed, said the presence of so many people in such a downpour was an expression of faith and generous sacrifice such as he had rarely seen. He said the family rosary means that husband, wife and children gather together for ten minutes a day, and are saying in different ways, "Dear God we love You, we depend on You, and cannot live without You." He continued, "The family rosary is the link that will bind together forever, God and the family."

Father Peyton emphasized that the three Roman Catholic bishops of Newfoundland, who were present, along with Chief Justice Sir Albert Walsh, and all the spiritual leaders in the province, shared in the conviction that the family rosary has the power and influence to unite with the Blessed Trinity every family that will make use of it. After a fairly lengthy and inspiring plea, the priest finished his address by imploring Almighty God to bless all present. A scheduled Benediction of the Blessed Sacrament was also canceled because of the rain. Sacred music for the occasion was provided by the popular Mount Cashel Band and the Roman Catholic Cathedral Choir.

Other Local News Events for the Year 1952

Jan. 8	Dr. Edward Wilson, Irishman, appointed Medical Superintendent at the General Hospital.
Jan. 12	Port au Port peninsula cut off from island as high tides and high seas carry bridge away.
Jan. 17	Westmount Community Center opened in St. John's.

Jan. 27	Premier Smallwood returns after three weeks absence.
Feb. 1	Premier Smallwood announces Boot and Shoe factory to be built in province.
Feb. 4	Three United States Navy submarines visit St. John's.
	New MacPherson Academy on Newtown Road, St. John's, officially opened.
Feb. 14	Premier Smallwood takes office as Minister of Natural Resources after resignation of Arthur Johnson.
Feb. 21	Worst snowstorm of the season ties up rail traffic across the island.
Mar. 3	Announced that firm of London, New York and Paris will take over James Baird Building on Water Street in St. John's.
Mar. 4	First group of Newfoundland WRENS sign up; Wilhelmina Rutherford, Rhoda Strong, Loretta Maloney and Louise Hall.
Mar. 6	First sealer leaves for the ice fields.
Mar. 7	James C. Thompson appointed Financial Advisor to the government.
Mar. 10	Premier Smallwood announces one million dollar Presswood plant to be built.
Mar. 12	Announcement was made that one thousand houses will be built in Gander.
Mar. 18	House of Assembly receives gift of table from Quebec and chairs from New Brunswick.
Mar. 23	Disabled sealing ship *Glenwood* towed into St. John's by *S. S. Kyle*.

Mar. 30	Fire at Corner Brook causes $1 million damage and leaves five families homeless.
Apr. 1	St. John's Municipal workers walk off the job.
Apr. 2	All members of Fortune Town Council resign.
Apr. 8	All members of Fortune Town Council with draw resignations.
Apr. 15	*M. V. Algerine's* third arrival from the ice fields.
	Premier Smallwood announces Lord Rothermore has accepted invitation to become Chancellor of Memorial University.
Apr. 16	Legislature has to adjourn sitting for want of a quorum, as opposition members walk out.
May 18	Three people killed in Labrador as plane flips, landing with wheels down on Cartwright Harbour.
May 21	Oliver (Al) Vardy named as Director of Tourist Bureau. Dr. Fred Rowe appointed Minister of Mines and Resources.
May 29	J. J. Mahoney retires as St. John's City Clerk. Honored with farewell banquet.
June 3	Swedish steamship *Tosca* arrives in St. John's with fire in hold.
June 5	E. B. Foran sworn in as new City Clerk, of St. John's.
June 10	Mrs. Elizabeth Rockwood charged with murder of her eleven-year-old son.
June 17	Premier Smallwood opens new Terra Nova Motors Building at Fort William.

June 30	Dr. A. G. Hatcher retires as President of Memorial University, succeeded by Mr. Ray Gushue, C. B. E., L. L. D.
July 4	Coldest July 4 on record—34. 4 degrees F.
July 8	Heat wave hits St. John's.
Aug. 4	Libel suits filed against CJON, the *Evening Telegram* and the *Daily News* by Mental Hospital doctors.
Aug. 10	Premier Smallwood announces sale of cement plant.
Aug. 15	Browning-Harvey's new bottling plant officially opened.
Aug. 21	Premier Smallwood in London, England, suggests formation of British company to develop Labrador.
Aug. 24	Family Rosary Crusade opens in Newfoundland.
Aug. 30	Governor General, Right Honorable Vincent Massey arrives for short visit to St. John's.
Sep. 11	Traffic lights installed for first time on Water Street.
Sep. 17	New Cottage Hospital at Fogo officially opened by Health Minister Chalker.
Sep. 22	Premier Smallwood has audience with the Pope in Rome.
Sep. 27	Commissioner William Dalziel of the Salvation Army lays cornerstone for new wing of Grace Hospital.
Oct. 6	U. S. Navy plane crashes at Argentia. Six men killed.

Oct. 9	Cornerstone of new Memorial University on Elizabeth Ave. laid by Lord Rothermere.
Oct. 17	Train derailment at Flat Bay in western Newfoundland. Engineer Ed Dunn and fireman Alec Robertson injured.
Nov. 1	Bishop Abraham opens new church at South River, C. B.
Nov. 5	New cottage hospital at Springdale officialy opened by Health Minister Chalker.
Nov. 11	New War Memorial at Spaniard's Bay unveiled by the lieutenant governor.
Nov. 13	Considerable damage caused to property as severe wind storm hits St. John's.
Nov. 27	Long distance telephone fees to mainland reduced by 50%.
Nov. 30	Fire at Corner Brook causes $1million damage and destroys fifteen business establishments.
Dec. 2	Bell Island miners vote to accept new wage and working agreement.
Dec. 6	Labor unions in Newfoundland decide to set up censorship board to control flow of undesirable Comic books.

Giant U. S. Bomber Crashes in Newfoundland—Radar Defense Test Turns to Tragedy.

On Wednesday March 18, 1953, a U. S. B-36 bomber crashed into the woods on the side of a hill near Burgoynes Cove, Trinity Bay, killing all twenty-three men on board.

During the war years of 1939-1945, the Americans and the R. C. A. F. had installed a sophisticated radar system to detect any aircraft approaching Newfoundland, and this system was still in operation in 1953. U. S. authorities decided to test the system, and one of their planes flying from the Azores to Gander was instructed to try to sneak in low enough to be undetected. The huge B-36 bomber was stationed in Newfoundland, so the crew were fairly familiar with the topography of the island, and knew that on the east coast the hills were only a few hundred feet high. They decided to come in at 1000 feet, hoping they would be below the radar scan. Unfortunately, they were unaware of a hill in the wilderness just north of Random Island that was 1500 feet high. As they came in in total darkness, they hit the hill with dev-astating results. On the north side of Smith Sound, Fred Bird and some friends who had come from Random Island the previous day, were just getting ready for breakfast at 4:00 a. m. It would soon be daylight, and they would spend the day cutting firewood in the area. Suddenly, a brilliant flash lit up the countryside, and several seconds later the sound of a loud explosion startled them. They knew what it had to be, and started walking through the thick woods towards the source. In less than two hours they reached the site, and were appalled at what they found: wreck-age and bodies lay scattered around, and a large piece of fuse-lage and some trees were still on fire. The aircraft, one of the largest in the world at that time, had ten engines, and had cut a swath 250 feet through the woods. There was no sign of life.

Fred Bird made his way back to the coast, and then trav-eled two miles by motorboat to Random Island, where he tele-phoned the RCMP in Clarenville. Fred's father, a telephone opera-tor at Lady Cove, phoned in a report to the *Daily News*. The other men remained at the crash site searching through the smashed trees, hoping to find survivors. There were none. By mid-morning, Pepperell Air Force Base had reported one of their planes missing on a flight from the Azores to Gander. The control tower had been advised that their last contact with the bomber was at 4:00 a. m. when they reported they were coming in at one thousand feet through fog. An RCAF search plane located the smoking wreckage just before noon, and two medics parachuted to the scene. The woodsmen gave them the bad news. In the meantime, ground search parties were on their way from Pepperell and Gander via Clarenville. From Clarenville they took several boats up through Smith Sound to the north shore, then a difficult trek through snow, woods, and steep hills. It took until midnight to reach the scene. The wreckage was still burning. The Mounties, led by Fred Bird, had gotten there much earlier, and noted that the number on the wreckage was the same as the number of the aircraft reported missing. The rescue people remained in the isolated area all night, and on the following day the search for bodies continued. All but two were found before nightfall, and the next day these two were located. Then the time-consuming task of getting the bodies back to Fort Pepperell began.

A clearing was cut so that a U. S. Coast Guard helicopter could land close by, and the victims were taken out, and flown the six miles to the small community of Monroe, on Smith Sound in Trinity Bay. It took twelve round trips. At Monroe, the remains were placed onboard a U. S. PBY Coast Guard sea-plane and an RCAF Canso, and flown back to Torbay Airport. From there, hearses were used for the transport to Fort Pepperell, where, after proper preparation, the twenty-three bodies were sent back to the United States for interment.

March 18th, 1953, was a sad day for the United Stated Air Force in Newfoundland. On that same day another U. S. bomber, this time a B-29, went down in St. George's Bay on the west coast of the island, killing all ten crew members. The plane was coming in for a landing at Harmon Air Force Base in bright daylight at 6:00 p.m. The approach to the runway is over the sea, and for some unknown reason, the plane didn't quite reach the airstrip, but went down into the water seventy-five feet deep. Wreckage and bodies were recovered the next day by divers. The ill-fated aircraft was based at Harmon and was part of the 52nd Air Rescue Squadron.

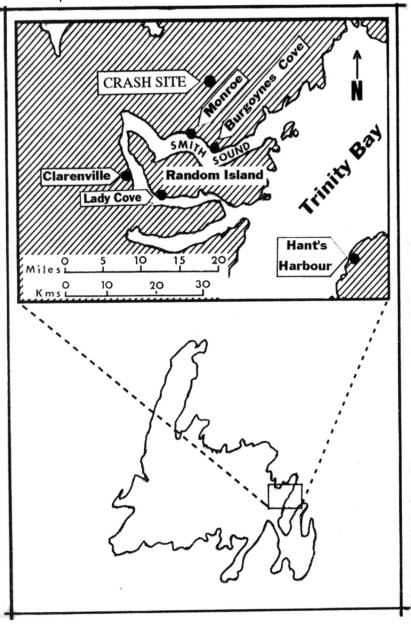

Map shows location of crash in 1953, eight miles north of Burgoynes Cove.

Other Local News Items for the Year 1953.

Jan. 1   Premier Smallwood leaves for Florida on health trip.

Jan. 3   Business premises of George Steward, Windsor, destroyed in fire that caused $150,000 damage.

Jan. 12   Warmest January 12 on record with 56 F.

Jan. 16   Fourteen U. S. soldiers killed in plane crash near Harmon Air Force Base, Stephenville.

Jan. 20   Premier Smallwood returns from Florida.

Feb. 13   Cabinet Minister Dr. Pottle announces glove factory to be built at Carbonear.

Feb. 21   Three military jets crash at Goose Bay. One pilot killed.

Feb. 24   *M. V. Ferryland* wrecked in the Caribbean. Crew safe.

Feb. 28   *M. V. Ice Hunter* is first ship to leave for the seal hunt this year under Captain Ernest Kean.

Mar. 6   Four other vessels leave for the ice fields.

Mar. 20   St. John's Municipal Council to provide fish market near Long Bridge replacing Steers Cove.

Mar. 26   *M. V. Arctic Prowler* is first ship home from the ice fields.

Mar. 28   New textile plant officially opened.

Apr. 6   Gordon Gruchy appointed Head of Economic Development.

St. John's Harbour with ice for eighteen days. Opened up by icebreaker *Saurel*.

Apr. 10   Legislature approves of Saturday holiday.

Apr. 29   Provincial budget introduced. Shows surplus of $6 million.

May 18   Premier Smallwood receives Honorary Degree Dr. of Laws at Acadia University.

May 21   Premier Smallwood and party leave to attend coronation in England.

June 7   Premier Smallwood and party arrive back from England.

June 17   Cornerstone for new Anglican Church laid at Grand Bank.

June 21   Rev. James J. Doody ordained to priesthood by Archbishop Skinner.

June 25   New boys home opened at Whitbourne.

June 29   Peter Pan Sales warehouse on Lime St., St John's, destroyed by fire.

July 1   Prime Minister St. Laurent arrives in St. John's on electioneering visit.

July 8   Major Peter Cashin resigns seat in legislature to run in Federal elections.

July 31   Rev. Fr. William. Carew appointed to staff of Vatican State Secretariat in Rome.

Sep. 15   New Masonic Temple opened and consecrated at Grand Falls.

Sep. 16   Fire at Stephenville. $125,000 damage.

Sep. 20   Schools opened today, two weeks late because of Polio epidemic.

Sep. 21	City carpenters walk out on strike.
Sep. 25	First Sisters of Service arrive in St. John's.
Sep. 28	189 cases of Polio reported to date. Twelve have died.
Sep. 30	Lady Baden-Powell, World Chief Guide, arrives in St. John's.
Oct. 2	Cornerstone for new St. Patrick's Convent, Patrick Street, laid by Archbishop Skinner.
Oct. 8	"Miss Canada", Cathy Archibald, arrives in St. John's and is welcomed by Mayor Mews.
Nov. 1	St. John's mayor Harry Mews re-elected unopposed. Fishery Convention opens at Bonavista.
Nov. 26	Newfoundland schooner *Dantzig* sank off Cape Breton. Crew rescued.
Dec. 6	Random Island causeway opened.
Dec. 11	Power outage hits St. John's as several poles blown down.
Dec. 20	First snowstorm for this season hits St. John's.
Dec. 25	Canada's first Christmas baby born to Mr. & Mrs. Roy Yetman of 17 New Gower Street.

Americans Donate Hospital at St. Lawrence

"The people of St. Lawrence and Lawn well-nigh accomplished the impossible "
— U. S. Vice Admiral Woolridge.

On June 6th, 1954, the American Government presented a fully equipped hospital to the people of St. Lawrence and Lawn, in appreciation of their outstanding work and the hardship they endured in rescuing one hundred and eighty-two U. S. sailors, after two warships, the *Pollux* and the *Truxton*, were wrecked on the Burin Peninsula during a severe winter storm in 1942. Two hundred and four men lost their lives in that tragedy. We covered the passing-over ceremony for the *Daily News*. We were brought to St. Lawrence in fine style on board the American warship *U. S. S. Caperton*, which sailed from Argentia on that Sunday morning. On board were the Lt. Gov. Sir Leonard Outerbridge; the Premier Joey Smallwood; several of his cabinet ministers and other VIP's, and of course, the press. All the guests on that ship were given documents certifying that we were now and henceforth honorary members of the crew of the *U. S. S. Caperton*, and entitled to all the rights and privileges as defined by MCMXLVII of the Articles for the Government of the Navy. We thought this was a nice gesture by the U. S. authorities. The ninety mile trip (145 km) across Placentia Bay took about three hours and I was amazed at

---

HONORARY CREWMAN

This is to certify that

MR. FRANK KENNEDY

IS NOW AND HENCEFORTH AN HONORARY
MEMBER OF THE CREW OF THE

USS CAPERTON (DD650)

AND IS ENTITLED TO ALL RIGHTS AND PRIVILEGES AS
DEFINED BY MCMXLVII OF THE ARTICLES FOR THE GOVERN-
MENT OF THE NAVY.

A. FARRIS, CDR, USN

COMMANDING

---

the speed of this huge ship. Standing at the stern, I could see the straight wake stretching back for miles, and I could hear the steady hum of the engines. It was truly a fascinating experience.

Waiting on the pier, as the warship arrived at St. Lawrence, were guards of honor from the U. S. Navy, the U. S. Marines, and the R.C.M.P., as well as hundreds of civilians from the area and a number of war veterans. As the dignitaries stepped ashore, they were welcomed by Mayor Farrell of St. Lawrence. Top brass of the United States present for the occasion included: U. S. Ambassador Douglas Stewart; U. S. Consul Barrett; the commanding officer of Fort Pepperell; and several U. S. rear admirals. The U. S. Army Band led a short march to the hospital site, where the ceremony took place outside the building in the presence of two thousand people from various parts of the Burin Peninsula. The flag of the ill-fated *U. S. S. Truxton* flew proudly from the roof of the hospital. The British and American national anthems were rendered by the band, as the scores of military personnel stood at attention and saluted appropriately, after which Rev. Fred Babb of St. John's read the invocation.

Captain J. S. Tracey, of the U. S. Navy, referred to the loss of the two ships, and the saving of 182 lives through the courageous actions of the residents of St. Lawrence and Lawn. Erection of this hospital, he said, was an everlasting expression of gratitude of the people of the United States, and a living memorial to the two hundred and four men who perished in the tragedy. Lieutenant Governor Outerbridge stressed the friendly feeling which existed between the Newfoundlanders and the Americans, and said it was a natural act for those who go down to the sea in ships, to aid those who had been victims of the perils of the sea. The governor said "...this wonderful gift makes all the closer, the happy relations between the two peoples." U. S. Vice-Admiral Woolridge said the people of St. Lawrence and Lawn well nigh accomplished the impossible, through their courageous action in rescuing the survivors of the 1942 disaster. He said both men and women had played their parts equally well. The U. S. Ambassador to Canada, Douglas Stewart, felt proud and privileged to be present to honor the people of the two settlements for their part in the rescue, and said this gift was only a small token of the respect which the United States has for the people of Newfoundland. The ambassador then passed over the keys of the building to Premier Smallwood. The premier thanked the ambassador for this fine gesture, and remarked on the continuing friendship between the people of the United States and Newfoundland. He then called for, "Three cheers for the United States, Hip! Hip!..." This was responded to enthusiastically by the two thousand people present.

Health Minister for the province Phil Forsey also spoke, and Mayor Farrell expressed thanks on behalf of the people of St. Lawrence and Lawn, and said no gift could be more appropriate. The flag of the *Truxton* was then lowered from the building and presented to Vice-Admiral Woolridge. It had been salvaged at the time of the wreck by Albert Beck. The ceremony concluded with the benediction by Rev. Fr. Mike Connolly, Parish Priest of St. Lawrence, and the playing of the Ode to Newfoundland. The *Truxton's* flag was later placed in a permanent location in the

Large picture mounted on sturdy brick base marks site of the old building. The New "U.S. Memorial Health Centre" is in background. *Photo by Glen Power.*

lobby of the hospital near a large plaque, giving in great detail the reason for the building's existence.

With the passage of several decades, and the enormous growth in the population of the area, a Royal Commission in 1989 found that a much larger hospital was now needed, and in 1993, a new hospital was opened just behind the old building. The latter was removed in 1994, and the site suitably marked with a large picture of the building sturdily mounted on a brick and concrete base with the inscription, "Site of the U. S. Memorial Hospital." The St. Lawrence Heritage Society commissioned Mr. Luben Boykov to design a bronze sculpture, and that very impressive work also stands near the site. It is entitled, "Echoes of Valor" and depicts a miner standing on a cliff, extending his hand to the outstretched arm of an oil-soaked American sailor. The people of St. Lawrence and Lawn will never forget the American sailors and I'm sure the reverse is equally true. The new hospital is fittingly named "The U. S. Memorial Health Center."

Impressive bronze monument entitled "Echoes of Valor" by Luben Boykov stands near the site of the old hospital. The sculpture was commissioned by the St. Lawrence Heritage Society. *Photo by Glen Power*

The Grounding of the two Warships and the Dramatic Rescue

"My God! We've hit a mountain!"
—Anonymous sailor on the *Wilkes*

The disaster occurred on February 18, 1942, when three U. S. Warships the *Truxton*, *Pollux* and *Wilkes* were traveling from Portland, Maine, to Argentia. It was wartime, and the small convoy was under blackout conditions and radio silence. The *Pollux* was a supply ship, bringing goods to the naval base at Argentia, and on board, besides the regular crew of one hundred and seventy-five men, were fifty-eight young navy recruits going to the Argentia base for training. The *Wilkes* was the flagship, or leader, and was the only ship with radar. Although this was her eighth trip from the States to Argentia, most of the crew this time were inexperienced sailors. The ships had been warned that German U-boats were operating in the area and could attack even in stormy weather, so the three ships maintained full speed ahead, and sailed in a zigzag pattern to avoid possible torpedoes. Normal night time navigation was done by the stars and compass, with the aid of a fathometer, an electronic device that would tell the depth of water under the ship. However, on the night they were nearing the Newfoundland coast, a snow storm was raging, and the skies had been overcast for the past forty-eight hours.

The captain of the *Pollux* wanted the *Wilkes* to change course and had the signal man flash a message to the flagship to that effect. He felt they were too close to shore. In the radar room of the *Wilkes*, the screen was constantly being monitored to keep track of the other two ships. Now a series of blips began appearing at the top of the screen, increasing in number until there were literally dozens of blips there. The radar operator called a senior officer and asked him what he thought of it. The officer said, "Surely there can't be that many ships out there in front of us! There must be something wrong with the radar. Have it checked when we get to Argentia." The fathometer read 200 feet of water underneath. Outside, the snow had turned to sleet, and the lookout, peering into the darkness, saw what he thought was a huge iceberg dead ahead. It was the snow covered cliffs of Lawn Head. He sounded the alarm, and immediately the engines were reversed and the rudder put hard over. The ship had slowed to five knots when it hit with a resounding crash. The captain ordered the searchlights manned and shone forward. They lit up the white cliffs. "My God!" someone shouted incredulously, "We've hit a mountain!"

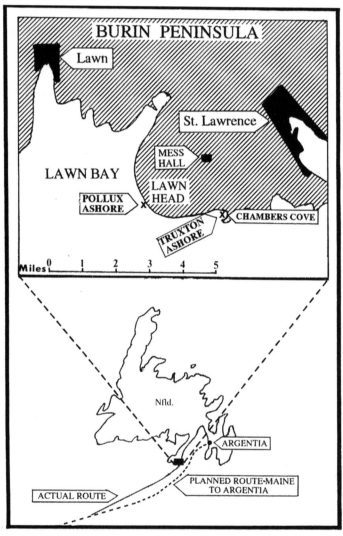

Map shows (lower section), how warships strayed from pre-arranged route to Argentia, and ended up on the rocks. Upper detail shows location of wrecks, etc.

The captain ordered the ships sirens sounded to warn the other ships, but they would not work. They were frozen up. He would have to break radio silence in this emergency and ordered the radio operator to quickly alert the ships of the danger. Although they were in a "radio silence" mode, all the receivers were left on, and could pick up transmissions without having the enemy home in on their positions. The operator found that the transmitter was not working either, as the outside antenna was covered with ice. Two sailors climbed a ladder on the smokestack and knocked the ice off the aerial, but this took another fifteen minutes, and their distress call was answered only by a radio station in Massachusetts. At least the radio was now working, but it was too late. The other two warships had run aground as well. It was just after 4:00 a. m. The *Wilkes* continued sending out the message, "*Wilkes* aground. Don't know which side [of Placentia Bay]." The mouth of that bay is 100 kilometers (60 miles) across and they didn't even know which side they were on! They were truly lost.

One mile east, the fifteen thousand ton *Pollux* had slammed ashore so violently that men in their bunks were thrown out onto the deck. The noise was so loud that some thought a torpedo had hit the ship. Others were sure they had collided with the *Truxton*. Several distress flares were fired into the dark sky, but this was a deserted area and no one on land saw them. Two miles further on, the *Truxton* ran aground in the relatively sheltered Chambers Cove. The back of the ship seemed to be in deep water, so the engines were put full astern. The warship moved back about ten feet and the propellers were torn off on the rocks. The stern swung around broadside to the wind and immediately the fuel tanks were ruptured, sending thousands of gallons of tar-like bunker-C oil out onto the sea between the ship and shore. On board the *Wilkes* it was noticed that only the bow seemed to be aground, so the captain ordered all cargo, munitions, etc. moved to the stern of the ship, and the oil pumped out of a forward fuel tank, with the hope that the stern would go down, and the bow come up. The idea worked, and three hours after grounding, the *Wilkes* slid slowly astern into deep water with only slight damage. The flagship hove to a half mile from the supply ship, but could do nothing to assist as the seas were far too rough to launch a boat. Five men from the *Pollux* had managed, with great difficulty, to get a raft ashore, but not without the loss of some of their shipmates in the vicious seas. Their life boats had been smashed to pieces by the huge waves. This ship's fuel tanks had also been punctured, and the men were covered with the thick, black oil. Some jumped overboard and attempted to swim ashore; others were swept overboard. Only a few made it. Many drowned. Some that did make it to shore froze to death on the spot. There was no beach here, just an outcropping of rocks, from which rose steep, ice covered cliffs three hundred feet high.

Back on the *Truxton*, their boats had also been smashed in the launching attempt, but the sailors had managed to get a line ashore and many were pulled to land in a breeches buoy, a chair-like device attached to a rope. There was a small beach here, but similar ice-covered cliffs all around. One sailor had some water-proof matches so a bonfire was started, using wooden crates that had been thrown overboard earlier and had washed ashore. But it was too late for some. Here too, several froze to death on the beach. When daylight came just after 5:00 a. m., five men scaled the cliff and found an old shed, eight by twelve feet. Inside was a quantity of hay and they lay down and covered themselves with it in an attempt to get warm. One of the sailors figured if that shed was there, then some houses should be close by, and he decided to look around. His name was Edward Bergeron. Unfortunately there were no houses close by, but he pushed on through the snow regardless, and after two miles, was ready to drop from exhaustion when he saw three men working at the top of a mine shaft. This was the fluorspar mine at St. Lawrence, and the men were Sylvie Edwards, Mike Turpin and Tom Beck. They ran to the man when they saw him staggering through the snow and were horrified to see he was covered with the black oil. "Where did you come from?" they asked. He could barely speak but managed to tell them he was from a warship ashore below the cliffs with over a hundred men on board, who needed help. Indeed, there were one hundred and fifty-five men on that ship when she struck, not to mention the two hundred and thirty-three on the *Pollux*, which he did not yet know about. The sailor was taken to the nearby mess hall, where there was a large hot stove, a welcome sight for him. The news was quickly spread around and, knowing it was too stormy to put out any boats, seven or eight men took off at once with ropes, and headed for the cove. There was no road; they had to beat their way through the snow. Several men came up from the mine to join the rescue party. Theo Etchegary came across the four men in the shed and told them to walk to the mine head; it wasn't far, he told them, and it was warm in the mess hall and there was lots of food and dry clothes there. They didn't want to leave their buddies on the beach, he was told. "If you stay here, you'll freeze to death," he warned, "and men are already on their way to help your buddies." They were led back to the mine building by Etchegary, who then headed back to the top of the cliff, where he met Tom Beck. They looked down at the shipwreck and were appalled at what they saw through the rain and sleet: the huge warship crashing up and down on the rocks, with forty foot waves smashing over the men hanging on to the railings. Some were jumping overboard and trying to reach a raft bobbing up and down in the oily mess. One man climbed onto it and fell off as a wave hit. He got back on. Theo saw his sixteen-year-old brother, Gus, and their father, Louis, down on the beach helping the survivors ashore. Tom Beck lowered Theo down the icy cliff after he had tied a rope around his waste.

At noon it was discovered that a second warship was ashore two miles further along the coast. Mine manager Horwood Farrell closed the mines for the day, and now scores of men from St. Lawrence and nearby Lawn, with horses and sleds, made their way to the two distressed ships. More men were lowered down the cliffs to assist getting the sailors ashore. Some Newfoundlanders even went out shoulder-deep in the freezing muck to drag in sailors who were unable to help themselves, but were kept afloat by their life jackets. A concerted effort was made to get the men up over the cliffs and back to civilization. It was a slow process. Each man had to be tied securely with a rope and gradually pulled up the two to three hundred foot cliff, with five or six men pulling on the ropes. It was found that when they were pulled up too fast, they were bruised and bleeding as they struck small outcroppings of rock on the way along. Most were semi-conscious at this stage and felt very little pain. Those who could still walk were led to the mine building, but most had to be taken by horse and sled. As the blackened, oil-soaked sailors began arriving at the mess hall, the women of the two settlements were alerted, and came with wash tubs, scrub-brushes, soap, food and warm clothes, leaving their teenage children to baby-sit the younger kids. District nurse Sadie Ash was called in and had her hands full attending the injured men. The sailors were stripped of the oil soaked clothes and placed on the mess hall tables, where the ladies began the arduous task of thawing out the half frozen bodies, and scrubbing the black oil from their skin. There was lots of hot water in the mess hall. When cleaned up, the men were given hot soup to bring them back to life.

Meanwhile, the coastal boat, *S.S. Kyle* had stayed in St. Lawrence over night to wait out the storm, and when the master, Captain Connors, heard about the groundings, he took the steamer out to the wrecks, but found he could do nothing there to help. He immediately brought the ship back to St. Lawrence and ordered the crew ashore with blankets and ropes and axes to help with the rescue operation. In the afternoon two U. S. war-ships, the *U. S. S. Brant* and the *U. S. S. Georges E. Badger*, arrived in St. Lawrence from Argentia, and naval doctors and medics were brought to the mine building to further treat the injured. They found the people of Lawn and St. Lawrence had brought much food to the hungry survivors, many leaving their own pantries empty. Several of the sailors had already been cleaned up, given warm clothes, hot soup, and then driven in trucks to various homes in St. Lawrence where they were put to bed. In the mess hall, the scrubbing continued. One of the ladies, Violet Pike, was becoming frustrated. "I can't seem to get the oil off this one!" she said aloud. "Ma'am," said the sailor, opening his eyes, "That's as clean as I get. I'm a black man." Violet was shocked. She had never seen a black man in her life. She smiled and put down the brush.

She was relieved to know that at least her work on this man was not in vain. One of the young ladies who helped the victims was nineteen year-old Ena Farrell. She was an office worker, but really had a "nose for news." She felt someone should be taking pictures of the historic happenings. Her mother had given her a five-dollar box camera and a few rolls of film two months earlier, for Christmas. She wanted to go to Chambers Cove and take some snaps, but felt she should not go on this day. I spoke with her in February, 1999, and she told me she thought at the time, that it would just not look right for a young lady to be taking photos of the horror that was going on. (She is now Mrs. Ena Farrell Edwards and is a prominent citizen of St. Lawrence.) The day after the disaster, she put on her skis, and with two other young ladies, went to Lawn Head and snapped the two wrecked warships. She also got shots of men in the process of recovering bodies. Later she photographed funerals of victims and burials in the cemetery at St. Lawrence. I have viewed more than twenty of her historic photographs, and it is my humble opinion that she would have been a top-notch news photographer, in the true sense of the word.

The day after the disaster, nineteen year-old Ena Farrell snapped this picture of the *U.S.S. Pollux*, broken in two, lying ashore off Lawn Head on the Burin Peninsula. *Thanks to Mrs. Ena Farrell Edwards for permission to use this photo.*

A few days after the tragedy, a lieutenant commander from the U. S. Navy appeared at her door and asked her to pass over the films she'd taken. She refused. He tried to persuade her that for the security of the U. S. Navy, she should comply with his request. She refused again, knowing full well that if she gave them up, even on loan, she would never see them again. Next day another visitor came, this time with an order from the base commander at Argentia, demanding the films. The commander wanted to impress on her the fact that if the enemy got their hands on these pictures, it could be detrimental to the U. S. Navy. She told him not to worry, she would make sure that would never happen. She said to tell the commander that she was sorry she could not comply with his order, but she had taken the pictures with her own camera, on her own film, and so they were hers, and that was that. Smart lady! A week after the disaster, the Associated Press representative in St. John's, Mr. Jeffries of the *Evening Telegram*, requested the films. It was agreed she would send him the films and he would have them developed and send them back to her. She told him they could publish whatever they wished. She sent the rolls to St. John's by registered mail. The store where Miss Farrell worked had a newsstand, and the following week, when she opened the weekly paper *The Montreal Standard*, she was surprised and delighted to see a double-page spread of her pictures with by-line. That was the first time she saw her photos. Later the pictures were returned to her, together with a cheque for $100. Again she was quite pleased, as it never occurred to her that she might get paid. She told me she went right out and bought a good folding camera.

The rescue operations at Lawn Head went on all day, and it was after midnight before the last of the one hundred and eighty-five survivors was hauled to the top of the cliff. When the "round-up" began (which took two days) trucks went about the community, picking up the sailors and taking them back to the warships in St. Lawrence Harbour. There were several stretcher cases, and as these were being carried aboard many young ladies, and older ones too, could be seen walking beside them holding hands with the injured men. A strong bond of friendship had developed in St. Lawrence on these two days.

Bodies kept washing ashore for weeks, and some of the two hundred and three victims were never recovered. Ninety U. S. Navy men were buried in a cemetery in St. Lawrence with full military honors, and forty-eight in Argentia. After the war, all bodies were exhumed and returned to the United States. Over the years, many of the survivors have returned to St. Lawrence to express their gratitude, and some St. Lawrence residents have visited survivors in the United States. In 1988 the town of St. Lawrence held a reunion, and forty United States citizens came to take part. Seventeen were actual survivors, and the others were relatives who wanted to meet the valiant Newfoundlanders who had saved their husbands and fathers. In 1992 an even bigger reunion took place. This time one hundred Americans came along. Again many were survivors, but this time several were retired officers and men of the *U. S. S. Wilkes*, the first of the three ships to run aground, and which managed to free herself. The mayor of St. Lawrence, Mr. Wayde Rowsell, and his wife went to New York in 1996 and again in 1998, and on both occasions visited relatives of the survivors. The Rowsells even visited the graves of the men who were originally interred at St. Lawrence and later removed to their final resting place in a Field of Honor in the United States.

Other Local News Items for the Year 1954

Jan. 1	Lieutenant Colonel and Mrs. Wiseman of the Salvation Army transferred to Toronto.
	Government grants one million dollar increase to teachers' salaries.
Jan. 5	Terra Nova Textiles opens new plant on James Lane.
Jan. 16	Mayor Mews announces poll tax for St. John's.
Jan. 27	Premier Smallwood says NAFEL must go.

Jan. 28	NAFEL ignores Smallwood's criticism.
Jan. 29	Denominational school system will continue, Smallwood declares.
Jan. 30	Heavy snowstorm blocks city streets.
Feb. 4	Fire destroys lumberyard at Chamberlains.
Feb. 6	Liberals announce they will not contest St. John's West seat in by-election. William Browne to run P. C.
Feb. 10	Colonel Effer, new leader of the Salvation Army arrives from Toronto. Two schooners lost in worst storm of the season. Crews saved.
Feb. 15	Smallwood denies going into business with Valdmanis.
Feb. 25	Smallwood predicts highway from St. John's to St. Anthony in the next four years.
Mar. 1	W. J. Browne new P. C. member for St. John's West, unopposed
	West Park Motors in Corner Brook destroyed by fire.
Mar. 6	Valdmanis gets Canadian citizenship.
	Sir Albert Walsh knighted by Pope Pius.
Mar. 12	St. John's City Council approves new water tax.
Mar. 16	Prov. government announces $600,000 slum-clearance program.
Mar. 18	*M. V. Newfoundlander* lost at sea. Crew rescued.
Mar. 22	Sisters of Mercy to operate Home for the Aged and Infirm.

Mar. 25	Premier promises fishery development in throne speech. Hollett calls throne speech, "fishy."
Mar. 30	Browne attacks Smallwood government. Challenges premier to produce details of new industries.
April 1	Higgins demands same.
Apr. 3	Fire destroys main office of DOSCO, Bell Island.
Apr. 5	Sealing vessel *James Spurrell* runs ashore near Codroy. Total loss. Crew saved. Sealing Vessel *Arctic Sealer* back from ice fields with 9000 pelts.
Apr. 8	Smallwood refuses to give report on economic development.
Apr. 9	*Arctic Prowler* back from ice fields with 11,000 pelts.
Apr. 12	Dunphy's Premises at Curling destroyed by fire. $150,000 damage.
Apr. 20	Report Russian trawlers operating on the Grand Banks.
Apr. 24	Valdmanis arrested for extortion.
Apr. 24	*M. V. Terra Nova* back from ice fields with 6700 pelts.
Apr. 26	Valdmanis charged with fraud. Remanded to prison. Gordon Higgins named his lawyer.
Apr. 28	Roland Parsons, Perry's Cove, charged with murder for shooting his wife.
	Smallwood denies report of large theft from government.

May 5	No bail for Valdmanis. Torbay Airport closed for five days due to fog.
May 7	Smallwood calls merchants, "Knuckle-headed fossils." Valdmanis granted $100,000 bail.
May 11	Valdmanis fails to get sureties. Still in jail.
May 13	First TV reception in St. John's. Freak reception from New Jersey.
May 15	Valdmanis out of jail. Sureties provided by Mrs. W. J. Higgins and Mrs. Dr. Kavanagh.
May 17	Valdmanis arrested again. Government lays civil charge to recover $270,000.
May 18	Valdmanis under house arrest at Newfoundland Hotel. Cecil King, Portugal Cove, walks home after seventeen days astray in woods.
June.1	Budget speech reveals surplus of $2,740,000. R. C. Bishops O'Neill and O'Reilly attend canonization ceremony of Pope Pius X in Rome.
Jun. 8	Valdmanis moved to Cochrane Hotel. Keough says $3 million to be spent onfishery development this year.
June 10	Browne tells the House Birch plant industry a failure.
June 16	Cinemascope comes to St. John's.
June 21	Pickersgill announces $300,000 fish plant for Badger's Quay.
June 29	Valdmanis appears in court and is again remanded.
July 2	City Council approves poll tax.

July 15	Local farmers report excellent hay crops.
July 16	Fishery on Burin Peninsula reported a failure.
July 22	Tooton Swimming Pool opened at Victoria Park in West End.
July 26	Smallwood says closing bars on Sundays would encourage bootlegging.
July 30	Thirty-three passengers injured as express and woods train collide near Glenwood.
	Government decided to close bars on Sundays.
Aug. 2	U. S. Navy aircraft crashes at St. Anthony. Eleven passengers escape with minor injuries.
Aug 6	Valdmanis preliminary hearing opens. Four witnesses heard.
Aug. 9	Valdmanis asks for trial by magistrate.
Aug. 10	Valdmanis committed to trial in Supreme Court.
Aug. 30	Irving Oil sets up business in Newfoundland.
Sep. 1	Fire destroys Nfld. Furniture Sales Building in St. John's. $150,000 damage.
Sep 3	City Council bans all further building on South Side Hills.
Sep. 11	Smallwood announces $650,000 loan to S. Lake and Mrs. M. Penney for Burgeo fish plant.
Sep. 13	Smallwood throws switch to start iron ore operations at Knob Lake.

Sep. 14	Smallwood announces $450,000 loan to fish plant at Fortune. Fifty foreign trawlers in port at St. John's sheltering from Hurricane Edna.
Sep. 16	Valdmanis convicted on $200,000 fraud charge. Remanded for sentence.
Sep. 18	Valdmanis gets four years.
Sep. 21	Railway service to take cars Clarenville to Gander started.
Sep. 30	Archbishop Skinner turns sod of St. Patrick's Mercy Home.
Otc. 1	Smallwood expelled from Press Club.
Oct. 12	Several injured as CNR bus and car collide.
Oct. 18	Fire destroys fish plant at Fortune.
Nov. 8	Record: five drunk drivers arrested in one day.
Nov. 10	Ayres' opens new supermarket at Churchill Square.
Nov. 14	Measles epidemic sweeps St. John's.
Dec. 8	Federal government says Newfoundland women lose $30,000 annually for failure to register new babies for Family Allowance.
Dec. 20	John C. Doyle predicts bright future for iron ore industry at Wabush.

Portuguese Fishermen Present Fatima Statue— Following in the Footsteps of Gasper Corte-Real

In an unprecedented display of affection and religious fervor, four thousand Portuguese fishermen marched to the Roman Catholic Cathedral in St. John's on May 27, 1955, and presented a statue of Our Lady of Fatima. Portuguese fishermen had been fishing on the Grand Banks forty-two years before John Cabot discovered Newfoundland, and in recent years, the "White Fleet" was a frequent visitor to St. John's, sometimes to shelter from storms, and always to take on supplies and fresh water. On such visits, many of the fishermen would invariably visit the Cathedral, half a mile from the harbour, and were always impressed with the way in which they were received by the local congregation. As a gesture of appreciation, it was decided by the Portuguese to make this presentation at the time when the Cathedral was celebrating its centenary, and was to be elevated to the status of Minor Basilica.

For several days, the three-and four-masted vessels had been arriving by the dozen, and on May 26, the "Mother Ship," the new hospital ship *Gil Eannes* entered the Narrows for the first of many visits. This was her maiden voyage, and her entrance to the harbour was greeted with a great blast of horn-blowing and signal flag displays, not only by the White Fleet, but also other ships in the harbour. From now on, this ship would drop anchor on the Grand Banks during the long fishing seasons, when thousands of Portuguese fishermen would be working in the area. If anyone became ill or was injured, hospital treatment would be available right there on the high seas. The statue of "The Lady of Fatima" had been on a small altar in the chapel of the *Gil Eannes*; on this Friday morning it was reverently taken out, together with the altar, which was decorated with fresh flowers from Portugal. In St. John's, the weather had been overcast and poor for a week, but as the statue appeared on the deck of the ship, the sun broke through in all its brilliance, as if to give heavenly assent to what was about to happen.

On the Navy dock in the west end of the harbour where the ship was berthed, four thousand Portuguese fishermen waited in silence as the statue was carried ashore. Their spiritual leader, Father S. A. Rosa, began singing the familiar "Ave Maria." In seconds, four thousand voices joined in, and the procession began moving to the streets of the city. Many of the fishermen were quite elderly, their faces weather-beaten from years on the Grand Banks. It was their last trip across the ocean, but they wanted to be present for this great event. Others were very young, mere boys, making their first trip to the fishing grounds; but they had heard about the friendly people of Newfoundland, and wanted to take part in this demonstration of affection. Most wore bright colorful shirts, which blended harmoniously with the hundreds of golden and red lanterns on poles held by the men forming a huge guard of honor. As the melodious voices echoed through this oldest city in North America, thousands of residents lined the streets and joined in the singing. The four altar-bearers were changed repeatedly along the way, to give as many as possible the privilege of taking an active part in the ceremony.

As the fishermen passed St. Patrick's Hall school on Queen's Road, the boys' choir standing in front of the building sang a hymn of welcome, and when the procession began entering the Cathedral, the choir there did the same. Inside the Cathedral, in front of the high altar, His Grace Archbishop Skinner stood facing the people and was visibly moved by this great expression of faith. In the sixteenth century, the great Portuguese explorer Gasper Corte-Real had walked in this very city and had honored the Blessed Virgin by naming the new-found bay "The Bay of Conception." Now, four hundred years later, the Portuguese people were still honoring her.

On this final leg up the center aisle of the church, the statue was now carried by officials of the Portuguese government and officers of the fleet. The lantern bearers formed a long orderly line in front of the white marble altar rails, as the archbishop formally greeted Father Rosa. The priest said he was presenting the statue on behalf of the commander of the White Fleet, and the government of Portugal. He brought the best wishes of the archbishop of Portugal, and greetings from the Government and people of his country, to the people of Newfoundland. Father Rosa thanked Archbishop Skinner for the kindness always shown to the Portuguese when they visited this province, and hoped the cordial relations would continue. He asked the archbishop to accept the statue as a mark of the continuing esteem and appreciation of the people of Portugal. Archbishop Skinner thanked the priest, and said the statue would be a holy and permanent link with the great country of Portugal. He prayed that the blessings of God would descend on the officials, officers and men of the fishing fleet and their families. Priests from twenty parishes

Statue of "Our Lady of Fatima" was presented to the Roman Catholic Cathedral by Portuguese fishermen in 1955. *Photo by Frank Kennedy*

watched as the statue was placed in a specially prepared alcove on the west side of the sanctuary. Today it remains as a permanent shrine to the Blessed Virgin Mary, who is believed to have appeared to children in Fatima, many years ago.

Full page photo in the *Daily News* showed some of the four thousand Portuguese fishermen at the start of their pilgrimage to the Cathedral. Dozens of ships of the "White Fleet" flew flags to celebrate.

One of the more impressive parts of the service happened at the closing, as the fishermen sang a goodbye hymn, and waved handkerchiefs in a reverent expression of farewell, as they slowly departed the building. Next day in the *Daily News* there appeared for the first time ever, a full page photo of a local news event. It was a picture of the thousands of fishermen on the pier, with the statue held high, and the lantern bearers forming the guard of honor. I got this shot by climbing onto the roof of a nearby building, where I had a clear view of the impressive scene. I was quite pleased that our editor gave the photo such prominence.

Sometime later I spoke with a friend of mine, a priest, who had attended the service at the Cathedral. He told me that a while back he had picked up a couple of Portuguese words, which he thought were some sort of greeting. Perhaps, "Good-day," or "God bless you." Anyway, after the service, as he stood on the steps, he thought he'd greet some of the fishermen, as they were leaving the church. He uttered the words, as he shook hands, and was delighted with the response. Everyone smiled, some even laughed, and everyone replied with words he could not understand, of course. He was a little curious, however, that no one repeated his actual greeting. Much later, he met a friend who was fluent in Portuguese, and asked him the exact translation. He was a little shocked to discover that he had been greeting the men with the words, "Long rubbers!"

Centenary of the Roman Catholic Cathedral, 1955

It took fourteen years to build the Cathedral of St. John the Baptist in St. John's, and in June, 1955, the 100th anniversary of the opening was celebrated with pomp and pageantry. Back then Bishop Michael Fleming, the fourth bishop of St. John's, responsible for the edifice, had to travel across the Atlantic by sailing vessel five times to get the deed to the land. When Fleming was made bishop in 1830, the one church in St. John's was an old rented building on Henry Street. The lease would run out in a few years, and the church was in a state of disrepair. In 1834 the bishop announced plans for a massive stone cathedral of unusual beauty and elegance, to be built on vacant land near Fort Townshend, if he could get possession of the lot. His efforts in that respect met with no cooperation from the local civil or military authorities, so he decided to plead his case in England. Each year for five years, he made the arduous round trip in a sailing ship. In those days, a one-way voyage across the Atlantic took several weeks. Finally, in April 1838, his persistence was rewarded when Queen Victoria made a grant of nine acres.

As soon as he returned, the land had to be surveyed and fenced as quickly as possible to secure ownership. Thousands of men, women and children rushed to the site, and in less than one hour, a five-foot-high fence was built around the 3.6 hectares of land. This was only the beginning of the enormous amount of manual labor carried out by the residents of the city and surrounding area. It was estimated that it would take two months to carry out the excavating for the huge 250 by 190 foot foundation. There was no heavy earth-moving equipment in those days, not even a truck or motorcar, and all the work had to be done with pick and shovel, and the material removed by wheelbarrow and horse and cart. Some of the ladies even used large aprons to carry away the gravel. People from all walks of life came to help their beloved bishop, and in an astonishing two days, the work was finished. More than five thousand tons of clay and rock had been removed! On another day the people took to the woods, ten miles away, and brought out four thousand pieces of timber, most thirty feet long, for the scaffolding.

It was originally planned to get the stone for the walls from Signal Hill and Kelly's Island in Conception Bay, but it was less expensive to bring it in from Ireland, and that is what was done. Once again, when the ships arrived, people of all denominations helped get the stone from the wharves up to the site. Fishermen and sealers not only contributed manual labor but also donations of money. So much so, in fact, that the bishop warned the men not to be too generous at the expense of their families. The massive two-ton granite cornerstone was set in place on May 20, 1841, and officially laid by Bishop Fleming. After that, construction proceeded slowly but surely. The bishop passed away in 1850, at the early age of fifty-seven, but not before celebrating the first mass in the partly finished building. He was obviously in a very poor state of health. Thirty years of hard work had taken their toll. His dear friend, Bishop John Mullock, took over and the building was finished by the summer of 1855.

Roman Catholic Cathedral celebrated its centenary in 1955 and was elevated to status of "Minor Basilica" *Photo by Frank Kennedy*

Several hundred St. Clare's nurses in full uniform and capes, marched from the hospital to St. Pat's Ball Park to attend the closing ceremonies. Daily News *Photo by Frank Kennedy*

Twenty thousand people attended the closing celebrations of the centenary of the Roman Catholic Cathedral at St. Pat's Ball Park in 1955. Daily News *Photo by Frank Kennedy*

For the consecration ceremony that year, bishops came from New York, Nova Scotia, New Brunswick and Toronto. The first High Mass was celebrated by Bishop Thomas Connolly of New Brunswick. One hundred years later, the parishioners celebrated for a week to honor this great event, and concluded with a giant parade through the city from St. Clare's Mercy Hospital to St. Pat's Ball Park. The parade had several brass bands and thirteen large colorful floats, each depicting an important event in the church's history, and showed real artistry and imagination in the construction. The first float had a scale model of the cathedral with three live actors representing the patrons of the church: the Blessed Virgin, Saint John the Baptist, and Saint Francis of Assisi. Another impressive float represented the opening of St. Clare's Hospital in 1922, and again had a live actor portraying Archbishop Roche outside the doors blessing the building. Inside were real hospital beds complete with live patients, being tended by doctors and nurses. With thousands of people representing dozens of societies, sodalities and parishes, the parade took one hour to pass a given point. It was under the direction of Major W. Collins and officers of the Newfoundland Regiment, who did an outstanding job of marshalling.

At the Ball Park, twenty-thousand people gathered for the closing ceremonies, by coincidence the same number that were present at the cornerstone laying one hundred and fourteen years earlier. His Eminence Cardinal McGuigan and several other distinguished prelates from many parts of Canada came for the celebrations in 1955. On this auspicious occasion, it was announced that in recognition of the centenary, Pope Pius XII had raised the status of the cathedral to that of Minor Basilica. "Basilica" means royal hall, and is rarely conferred. The title is given only to certain churches outstanding for their historical, artistic and ecclesiastical importance.

Other Local News Events for the Year 1955

Jan. 1   First baby of the year born to Constable. and Mrs. R. Noseworthy.

Jan. 4   United Towns Electric Company announces they will harness Manuels River for power development.

Jan. 5   Family Allowances reach $62,000,000 since confederation.

Jan. 6   Mountainous seas destroy property all over Avalon Peninsula. Wharves and stages at the Battery swept out to sea.

Jan. 26   Fire destroys business premises of City Service Company and The Arcade.

Jan. 27   Heavy snowstorm hits St. John's.

Jan. 29   Another heavy snowstorn hits city. Streets blocked.

Jan. 31   A third snowstorm hits city. Seven-foot-high drifts.

Feb. 10   Four killed in plane crash at Goose Bay.

Feb. 26   A. N. D. company uses first wood from Labrador.

Mar. 8   *M. V. Algerine* first ship to the ice fields.

Mar. 18   Four killed as car hits bus near Octogan Pond. Inspector and Mrs. Mahoney and Mr. & Mrs. Leonard.

Mar. 21   U. S. Airforce plane crashes into St. George's Bay. Two airmen missing.

Mar. 23   *M. V. Algerine* reports 10,800 pelts on board.

Mar. 30	Smallwood says third paper mill is a reality.
Mar. 31	Number of seats in House of Assembly increases from twenty-eight to thirty-three.
Apr. 2	*Arctic Prowler* first ship back from ice fields. 20,000 pelts on board.
	Smallwood loans mainland mink ranchers $200,000.
Apr. 7	Smallwood says third paper mill is a certainty.
Apr. 12	St. John's Harbour blocked by ice. Shipping trapped.
Apr. 13	Crew of sealer *Terra Nova"* earn $222 each.
Apr. 14	Offshore winds clear ice from harbour.
Apr. 18	Severe snowstorm blocks city traffic for eighteen hours.
Apr. 19	Provincial budget brought down. $1 million surplus. Government to borrow $16 million.
Apr. 21	Smallwood announces loan of $500,000 to establish Adler's Chocolate Factory at Bay Roberts.
Apr. 25	Critical situation on Bell Island as ice blockade continues.
Apr. 26	Ice breaker *Saurel* reaches Bell Island with mail and food.
May 2	Late snowstorm blocks city streets.
Mar. 5	*M. V. Placentia* hits iceberg. No serious damage.

May 20	Last of three Marconi poles at Mount Pearl demolished.
May 23	Three men killed at Port aux Basques as train hits truck.
May 27	New Portuguese hospital ship *Gil Eannes* arrives in St. John's.
June 2	Judge rules sleeping in car not cause for drunk driving charge.
June 13	Rennie's swimming pool will not open this year because of sanitary condition.
June 27	Roman Catholic Cathedral raised to status of Minor Basilica.
July 16	Smallwood opens Orange Association Convention at Springdale.
July 18	Narrow escape for family as fire destroys home on Richmond Street.
Aug. 8	Seven people left homeless as fire destroys home of Charles Taylor, Topsail.
	Strawberries selling at $3.00 per gallon.
Aug. 10	Holyrood fishermen earn $90 in one day fishing squid.
Sep. 1	St. John's Harbour crowded with ships sheltering from hurricane Edith.
Sep. 2	DOSCO opens new conveyor belt system on Bell Island.
Sep. 6	First tests CJON television big success.
Sep. 22	Heavy damage by severe wind storm.
Oct. 18	Smallwood tells Ottawa, Newfoundland needs one billion dollars for development.

Nov. 14   Schooner *Mable & Dorothy* wrecked at
               Horse Islands. Seven crew all lost.

Dec. 12   Severe snowstorm hits city.

Dec 13   Pikersgill buys local schooner.

Dec. 20   *M. V. Susan Jones* lost at sea. All crew saved.

Dec. 29   Smallwood leaves for holiday in West
               Indies.

Dec. 30   Mr. John O'Toole, seventy-nine, retires after
               sixty-two years with the *Daily News*. He
               boasted that he never worked a day in his
               life, in all his time with the *News*. (He was
               on permanent night shift as a linotype
               operator.)

Some Local News Events of the Year 1957

Jan. 2   Valdmanis paroled, flees to Montreal.

Jan. 3   Government to close old sanitarium on
               Topsail Rd.

Jan. 9   Heavy snowstorm disrupts city traffic.

Jan. 18   *Cabot Strait* runs aground. Crew Safe.

Jan. 21   Coal shortage on South Coast.

Jan. 24   Heavy rain causes flooding and damage to
               many city homes.

Jan. 31   Portugal Cove blocked with ice. Bell Island
               ferry uses Brigus.

Feb. 1   Frank Johnson found guilty of manslaugh-
               ter. Gets ten years.

Feb. 5   Ferry *Kippewa* runs aground at Bell Island.

Feb. 11   Local doctors claim problem with tubercu-
 -             losis still great.

167

Feb. 14	Hare Bay North business premises destroyed in fire. $100,000 damage.
Feb. 21	Smallwood says nothing can take the place of the Union Jack.
Feb. 28	Fort Pepperell abolishes 200 jobs.
Mar. 4	St. John's Board of Trade claims city needs new railway station.
Mar. 7	Sealing ships sail for the ice fields.
Mar. 11	Island of Newfoundland completely surrounded by ice. All shipping halted.
Mar. 12	Well-known Christian Brother P. M. Eagan passes away.
Mar. 19	Sealing ship *Beater* sinks in Gulf. Crew safe.
Mar. 25	London Theater Company stages their final show in Newfoundland.
April 1	W. J. Browne says Smallwood is political spendthrift.
	C. N. R. express bogged in snow on the Gaff Topsails. One hundred and thirty-five passengers marooned.
May	Fishermen's Insurance announced.
	Newfoundland is to get fourth Supreme Court judge.
	Mrs. Ramsay Smallwood and pilot killed in helicopter crash at Russwood Ranch.
June	Bell Island ferry service discussed in the House. Said to be unsatisfactory.
	W. J. Brown and Jim McGrath elected in federal elections as Diefenbaker defeats St. Laurent.

July	Apostolic delegate visits St. John's. United Church to build $1 million dollar school in St. John's.
	Canadian Javelin awarded $176 million timber rights.
August	BRINCO issues encouraging report. *Northern Ranger* and *Springdale* run aground.
	P. C. leader Malcolm Hollet charges Two Way Stores make exorbitant profit from sale of food to government. (One of the cabinet ministers is co-owner with his brother.)
September	Churchill Falls declared world's largest power potential.
	Report of poverty and privation comes from Southwest coast.
October	Report of Krupp investigating Javelin iron ore deposits. C.N. R. embargo goes into effect as strike threatened.
	Supplies of Asiatic Flu vaccine arrive in city.
	Authorities discuss "Brookfield Bridge" where numerous accidents have happened.
November	Concrete Products Company strike ends after three months.
	Mayor Harry Mews re-elected unopposed.
	Gloomy outlook for new industries. Machine plant and glove plant may have to close.
December	Heavy winds disrupt local shipping operations.
	City lawyer Derick Lewis ordered to pay fines for fifty parking tickets.
	Local controversy over St. John's Harbour improvement plan.

The Ice Storm of 1958—Avalon Peninsula Paralyzed

On Saturday, March 1, 1958, a severe sleet storm hit the island, and caused extensive damage on the Avalon Peninsula. Some areas were without power for several weeks. First, the heavy ice-encrusted power lines sagged and parted with lightning-like flashes. Then the telephone and power poles and transformers came crashing to the ground; finally, the VOCM radio transmitter mast and the CBC's 300-foot-tower in Mount Pearl toppled and fell. Hundreds of stately trees were destroyed. The freezing rain began in the St. John's area Friday evening, and by 3:00 a. m. on Saturday, some sections of the city began experiencing power failures. By 9:00 a. m. the whole city was without electricity, and as the sleet continued building up all day, it became obvious that we were in serious trouble. Power lines and poles were falling all over the city. On Torbay Road twenty-six poles came down, and on Bell Island a staggering four hundred poles lay on the ground in a mass of tangled wires and transformers. The mines there had to shut down. People with battery radios rushed to stores to get fresh batteries and keep abreast of the news. Then, during the day, VOCM and CBC radio went off the air as their transmitters went out. Fortunately CJON radio remained on the air, thanks to their own emergency generator, and VOWR also broadcast ice storm news. At the city hospitals, emergency lights came on, but as these were operating on battery power they dimmed and went out after only a few hours. At the Grace Hospital, C.E.O. Brigadier Janes was thankful there were no emergencies, although six babies were born during the day. St. Clare's Hospital was lucky in that all the kitchen stoves were operated by gas, so hot meals were always available. Seven babies were delivered in that hospital during the first twenty-four hours.

On Saturday night, the bad news was announced by the power company. They were doing all they possibly could to restore power, but it would be several days, maybe a week, before even the city was back to normal. Outlying areas would take much longer. Most of the Avalon Peninsula was out. Authorities at

Fort Pepperell responded to the crisis and supplied huge generators to the three city hospitals. Hundreds of U. S. military personnel lived in various sections of St. John's with their families, and they were allowed to move back to the base for a week. Pepperell had an independent powerhouse, and all wires were underground, and unaffected by the sleet. More than six hundred men, women and children moved in. At 8:00 a. m. on Sunday the Glenbrook Lodge, a home for single mothers on Torbay Road, put out a call for help. They'd had no heat or light for over twenty-four hours, and had twenty-five infants in their care, including one sick child. The Grace Hospital quickly responded, and sent their ambulance to pick up the children. The nursery at the Grace was already full, thanks to the six new arrivals, but space was provided in the nurses' library. The staff of Glenbrook came along and set up quarters there for the little ones, and remained to look after them. On Sunday, stores on Water Street (the main shopping district at that time) were allowed to open, and were flooded with customers seeking oil heaters, oil lamps, candles and bags of coal for their grates and kitchen stoves. One supplier sold forty-nine

On Torbay Road, twenty-six poles came down. This scene was repeated dozens of times throughout the city. Daily News *Photo by Frank Kennedy*

tons of coal in bags by noon that day. Bowring Brothers sold more than twenty-seven thousand candles and numerous oil lamps and lanterns. At Neyle-Soper's Hardware just across the street, when we visited the area, the store was packed with customers and there was a lineup outside. Several young boys with entre- preneurial spirit bought candles downtown and sold them door to door at a substantial profit. People could be seen with all sorts of containers going to service stations to buy kerosene oil. The gas pumps had to be operated by hand, a very slow process, and it was not uncommon for drivers to wait in line for an hour for a fill-up. The Towne and Country Restaurant on Water Street, owned by Barney Williams, had never before opened on a Sunday, but it did on that day, and like other restaurants in the city, served only cold sandwiches and soft drinks. Delicatessen stores had a big run on cooked meats, as customers sought ingredients to make their own lunches. All these stores were sold out by noon. At the old Newfoundland Hotel, lanterns were hung at either end of the many corridors, and guests were given candles for their rooms. In the dining room, at night, all the tables were lit by candlelight. That may sound very romantic, but the menu was not very erotic— cold sandwiches and room-temper- ature milk. By Monday the situation there had improved. Several oil stoves were put into service and hot soup and pork chops were available, as well as tea and coffee.

Fire department authorities were very worried. Not only were thousands of residents using candles in their homes, but most of the telephones were out because the lines were down, and this would make it difficult to get a call in to a fire hall. They did respond to six minor fires during the blackout, caused by lighted candles, but no serious damage resulted. Telephone and power company linesmen worked around the clock, with help from outside, and their first priority was getting the city hospitals back on line. At 3:30 p.m. on Sunday, sighs of relief could be heard as power was restored to the St. Clare's area. We were lucky enough to live near the hospital at the time, and were among the few dozen homes which were first to get power back in the city. Over the next few days, electricity and telephone service was

A transformer lies on the ground as in the background, ice covered wires sag from pole.

Emergency generators were loaned to the three city hospitals by authorities from Fort Pepperell.

CBC's 300-foot radio transmitter mast at Mount Pearl crashed to the ground under the weight of the ice. Daily News *Photo by Frank Kennedy*

gradually restored, but it took nearly a week before the city was back to normal. Thanks to the co-operation of Wesley Radio (VOWR), the CBC were able to use their transmitter tower on Nagle's Hill, and get their radio station back on the air. It took several weeks to build the new tower at Mount Pearl.

Bell Island was in desperate straits. Not only were the mines closed down, throwing hundreds of men out of work for two weeks, but kerosene oil was in very short supply and lamps and oil stoves were scarce. The population then was over ten thousand. Special trips were made by the ferries from Portugal Cove with tanker trucks of oil, and other badly needed supplies. The Goulds, the Southern Shore, and most of Conception Bay were without power for two weeks, and other outlying areas on the peninsula didn't see light for a month.

Memorial University Opened by Mrs. Eleanor Roosevelt

"Only two greater things have happened to Newfoundland."
—Premier Joey Smallwood

On Monday, October 9, 1961, Thanksgiving Day, the new Memorial University Campus in St. John's was officially opened by Mrs. Eleanor Roosevelt, wife of the former president of the United States, Franklin D. Roosevelt. It was a big day for Newfoundland, and especially for Premier Joey Smallwood, who had turned the first sod ten years earlier, on May 27, 1951. He declared the day a public holiday and invited VIPs from all over the world, and most of them came. The Prime Minister of Canada, Honorable John Diefenbaker came and was given an honorary degree. The President of the United States, John F. Kennedy, was invited, and sent Mrs. Roosevelt in his place. Invitations were sent to each of the forty-two universities in Canada, and forty-one sent their chancellors or vice-chancellors. Smallwood chartered a large airliner and brought in dignitaries from Europe, South Africa and Australia, including the duke of Devonshire, Lord Beaverbrook, Sir Eric Bowater, Honorable Norman Manley, premier of Jamaica, and

At Neyle-Soper Hardware on Water Street, customers waited outside the already filled store to buy emergency supplies. Across the street Bowrings' sold twenty-seven thousand candles in one morning. Daily News *Photo by Frank Kennedy*

With power off for several days, gasoline had to be pumped by hand, a slow process. Here, cars line up on Hutching's Street for a fill-up at Harry Summers, service station. Daily News *Photo by Frank Kennedy*

Dr. A. L. Cortesco from the University of Coinbra in Portugal. Smallwood rounded up fourteen hundred students from all parts of Newfoundland and Labrador, and brought them to the city, at government expense, to take part in the largest parade ever seen in the province. Franklin D, Roosevelt was considered by many to be the greatest president since Lincoln and when Mrs. Roosevelt arrived at Torbay Airport, thousands were on hand to give her a true Newfoundland welcome. The red carpet was rolled out to the steps of the aircraft, and the Lieutenant Governor, Honorable Campbell MacPherson, greeted the lady as she stepped off the plane. Two hours later, the Prime Minister, Honorable John Diefenbaker, arrived and was welcomed by Premier Smallwood. Again, thousands witnessed the event.

The high point of the two-day celebration came as Mrs. Roosevelt presented the keys of the buildings to the new Chancellor, Mr. Roy Thompson, a highly respected Canadian newspaper magnate. This ceremony took place in the spacious new gymnasium where seventeen hundred people had gathered to watch. Premier Smallwood was chairman, and said it was a great honor to have so many distinguished guests present on this momentous occasion. Referring to the opening of the new university, he said, "Only two greater things have happened to Newfoundland. The first was when John Cabot discovered the island, and the second was Confederation."

In introducing Mrs. Roosevelt, Smallwood said she was a great humanitarian and tireless worker for good causes, and we were delighted to have her with us. After an eloquent speech, Smallwood handed the keys to Mrs. Roosevelt, with the request that she present them to the chancellor. As Mrs. Roosevelt arose, there was prolonged applause, and she said it was a great pleasure for her to represent President John F. Kennedy at this time, and she was greatly honored to be a guest of the government of Newfoundland. She said her late husband had often fished and hunted in eastern Canada, and had a great affection for the country. As she presented the keys to Chancellor Thompson, there was a tremendous ovation. Mr. Thompson declared it was a great honor to receive these keys, symbolic of the University buildings, from such a distinguished personage. He noted he was probably one of the least educated Chancellors in the world, having never attended a university. However, it was his belief that a business-man has a contribution to make, equal in degree, with those of scholars, statesmen and soldiers. Referring to Newfoundlanders who died in two world wars, the sixty-seven-year-old chancellor said there was a gallant sacri-fice behind the university, and no better memorial could have been conceived to honor their memory.

Canada's Prime Minister, Hon. John Diefenbaker, is welcomed by Premier Smallwood as he arrives for the official opening of the new Memorial University campus in 1961. Daily News *Photo by Frank Kennedy*

Mrs. Eleanor Roosevelt, centre, arrives at Torbay Airport to officially open
the new Memorial University campus in 1961. She was welcomed by
Lt. Gov. Campbell MacPherson. Daily News *Photo by Frank Kennedy*

Bright sunshine greeted the day of the big parade. A reviewing stand was erected at the entrance to the campus on Elizabeth Avenue, and more than two hundred guests were seated, as the proud students marched past. Mrs. Roosevelt was guest of honor, and sat between Prime Minister Diefenbaker and Premier Smallwood. At the rear of the stand, flags of the ten provinces fluttered in the gentle westerly breeze. Nearby, the Royal Jamaican Band alternated with the U. S. Navy Band in providing lively music before the start of the parade. Smallwood had arranged to have large banners with place-names provided to the students, and these were proudly displayed as the parade passed in front of the dignitaries. It took nearly an hour for the fourteen hundred participants to pass a given point, and sixteen bands provided appropriate martial airs for the marchers. At that time all students wore school uniforms, and the assortment of bright colors added variety and class to the event, which was guided by members of the Royal Canadian Legion. In the evening the government hosted a gourmet dinner for one thousand guests, in the gymnasium of the Holy Heart of Mary School, now converted into a huge banquet hall. Mrs. Roosevelt was presented with a beautiful fur stole by the premier on behalf of the Newfoundland people. The following day a special convocation was held, and for the first time, the university conferred honorary degrees. Receiving these degrees as well as the prime minister and Mrs. Roosevelt, were such distinguished and well-known persons as Most Rev. Patrick J. Skinner, Roman Catholic archbishop of St. John's; Right Reverend John A. Meaden, Anglican bishop of Newfoundland; Right Reverend Hugh A. McLeod, moderator of the United Church of Canada; Sir Leonard Outerbridge, former lieutenant governor; Newfoundland-born poet, Edwin J. Pratt, and Premier Smallwood. Memorial University College was first opened in 1925, but it was not authorized to confer degrees. Over the years many of the graduates would go to Canada to get their doctorates, and often would not come back. This always worried Joey Smallwood, and when he brought Newfoundland into confederation in 1949, one of the first pieces of legislation his government enacted was to raise the status of Memorial College to that of a degree-conferring university.

With the Arts and Administration Building as a background, the longest parade in the history of Newfoundland passes the largest reviewing stand during opening celebrations of the Memorial University campus. Daily News *Photo By Frank Kennedy*

Governor Alderdice officially opened the University College in September, 1925, and at that time the enrollment was fifty students with four teachers, including the President, Mr. John L. Paton. At confederation there were 307 students, and by the time they moved into the new campus in 1961, the university had 1907 students. As the enrollment grew, so did the campus, and several new impressive buildings were added over the years. In 1966 the enrollment stood at 4762 in eight buildings, and in the peak years 1992-93, there were an incredible 18,632 students registered. With increasing tuition fees and private colleges opening in the St. John's area, not to mention out-migration of thousands per year, enrollment declined somewhat, and in 1999 stood in the fifteen to sixteen thousand range.

Iron Ore Mining Begins in Western Labrador—Death Knell for Bell Island

On Tuesday, July 10, 1962, with a tremendous blast that could be heard for miles, Joey Smallwood detonated seventy-four tons of explosives, and blew the top off a mountain. It was the official opening of the Carol project in western Labrador and the start of the Smallwood iron ore mine. We covered the event for the *Daily News*, and just getting to the site in Labrador City was an interesting adventure in itself. All expenses were covered by the Iron Ore Company of Canada. The premier, several government and company officials, and the press boarded a 737 jet aircraft at Torbay Airport the previous day, and were flown nonstop to Sept-Iles, a Quebec port on the gulf of St. Lawrence. From the airport there, we were taken to a fine hotel and checked in just in time for dinner. Next morning we were driven the short distance to the railway station, having been informed the previous night that breakfast would be served in the dining-car of the train that would take us the 160 miles to Labrador City, the site of the mine.

As I sat at the table in the diner, the first thing I noticed was a tall vase of carnations. Having often traveled on the "Newfie Bullet," and knowing full well how shaky that train was, it occurred to me that this vase had to be somehow fastened to the table. I picked it up and was surprised to find it was not. Well now, I thought, when this train starts moving, I'd better be ready to grab this vase before it falls over and deposits cold water on my lap. The very dignified waiter passed me a menu. As I was studying it, I noticed through the corner of my eye, something moving outside the large picture-window. Looking up I saw, to my great surprise, it was the railway station moving away. Incredible! There was no sensation of movement whatsoever. This railway, The Quebec North Shore and Labrador Railway, was wide-gauge and had been built only two years earlier, at a cost of a quarter billion dollars, and was smooth as silk. I enjoyed my breakfast of juice, cereal, bacon and eggs; and the fear of a wet lap evaporated as the landscape went rushing by. After that fine meal we went back to a first-class coach to enjoy the view. We passed such places as Nipisso, Lika, Waco and Eric while still in Quebec. When we crossed the border, after 130 miles, we were into "The Big Land,"—the last pristine wilderness in North America—Labrador! Beautiful countryside on this fine summer day, shimmering blue lakes and spruce-covered hills . Someone said it was the kind of land wherethe hand of man had never set foot. Suddenly blackness! My God, have I gone blind? No, there are dim lights in the ceiling of the car. Someone said, "A tunnel." Yes, we had gone into a dark tunnel at forty miles per hour. Startling, to say the least. Years earlier, builders of the railroad had determined it was more practical to go through this mountain than around it. By the time our eyes started getting used to the dimly-lit car, we were back in the bright sunlight. It happened again, but this time we were rounding a gentle curve, and could see ahead of us the black hole in the mountain that we were about to enter.

We passed through Embar, Pitaga and Drylake, and for about an hour we were traveling on the shores of beautiful Ashuanipi Lake. That body of water is forty miles long. I thought, "Boy, what a place to wet a line. It must be teeming with fish." I noticed the evergreen trees (spruce and fir) were different from those on the island. They are very tall and thin (like me!). The lower branches seemed to be stunted in growth. They were not as long or thick as the island trees. It would be hard to find a real good Christmas tree here, I felt. We arrived in Labrador City at 4:00 p.m. As our train slowed down, we saw hundreds of people, mostly schoolchildren, Girl Guides and Boy Scouts at the station, anxiously waiting for the premier. Smallwood did not disappoint them. He was enthusiastically shaking hands with the children even before Mines Manager Dr. A. E. Moss extended a hearty welcome. Joey then addressed the children at the railway station. He told them they should be proud of being a part of this growing community and of living in a great age of development. He said they should write their buddies to tell them what a wonderful place Labrador City is and will become.

That night two hundred guests attended a banquet at the Sir Wilfred Grenfell Hotel, in nearby Wabush, and Smallwood was guest of honor. Dr. Moss chaired the affair, and the first President

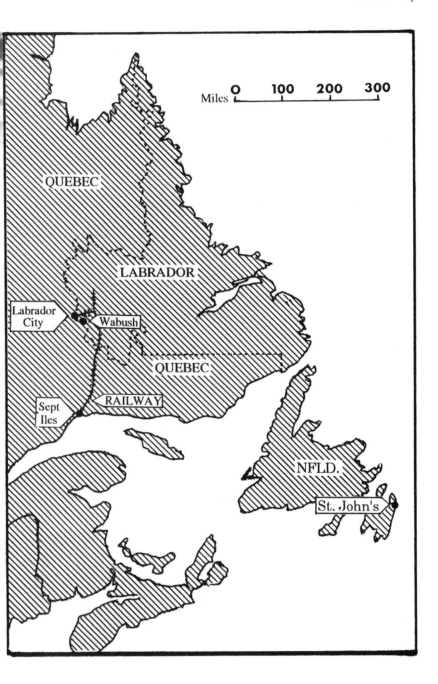

Map shows location of mining areas in Western Labrador.

Driverless trains look scary as they pass by with no one in the cab. They are completely automated, and transport iron ore five and a half miles from the mines to the crusher building. *Photo Courtesy I.O.C*

Two workmen, centre left and upper right, are dwarfed by the huge machines in the crusher plant in Western Labrador. *Photo Courtesy Wabush Mines*

of the Iron Ore Company, Mr. G. M. Humphrey, in introducing Joey, praised him for his great leadership. Smallwood spoke for forty-five minutes and said he expected that in a few years fifteen thousand men would be employed here, and the population of Labrador City would grow to one hundred thousand. He expected fifty million tons of ore concentrate a year to be produced. He said the cost of this Carol project, including the $250 million for the railway, was $800 million, one of the greatest gambles Canada has even seen. Referring to criticism of too many mainlanders working in Labrador, Smallwood said right now there were one hundred thousand Newfoundlanders working on the mainland of Canada, but only two thousand mainlanders working in all of Newfoundland. He concluded by adding that there would be a terrible row if workers were restricted to finding jobs in their own provinces. The Labrador Glee club provided entertainment, and were loudly applauded for their rendition of Newfoundland folk songs.

Next day came the "Big Bang." Workmen had spent three weeks drilling one hundred holes in a solid mountain of ore, some as deep as fifty feet. The explosive used was Hydromax, a new product developed by the Iron Ore Company. It was just as powerful as dynamite but not nearly as dangerous. When Smallwood pushed the plunger, and the mountain blew its top, the few people left in Labrador City, seven and a half miles away, heard a loud, thunder-like roar. Most of the residents were already at the site witnessing the spectacle. That blast loosened one hundred and sixty thousand tons of ore. In the mining industry, bigger is definitely better. After blasting, gigantic electric power shovels moved in and took up to twenty tons of ore in one shovelful, and dump it into rubber-tired ore trailers. Each of these mammoth machines carried one hundred tons of ore to a waiting ore train. And that was something else! No driver! Automated trains! Back in 1962! It was weird watching a Diesel locomotive pulling fifteen cars, each loaded with one hundred tons of ore, passing by with no one in the cab. There were four of these trains working simultaneously, bringing the ore five and a half miles to the crusher building. After processing, the iron concentrate was

Fifteen cars on each train, each carry one hundred tons of iron ore. There were four such trains. *Photo Courtesy I.O.C.*

Premier Joey Smallwood (in white hat) detonates seventy-four tons of explosives, a half mile away, to officially open mining operations in Western Labrador in 1962. Daily News *Photo by Frank Kennedy*

loaded on trains and brought down to Sept-Isles for loading aboard ore-carriers ships.

June 22, 1965, saw the dedication and start-up of Wabush mines, just a few miles south east of Labrador City, and by 1998, Labrador was producing 55% of all the iron ore mined in Canada, twenty-two million tons a year. It was less than half the tonnage Smallwood had predicted; nevertheless at that rate of production, it is estimated there is enough iron ore in western Labrador to last more than a hundred years. In 1999 the population of Labrador City had reached 8455, with thirteen hundred employed at the mines. As intimated in the sub-head of this story, the opening of these mines was bad news for Bell Island. Just a year earlier, in 1961, the work force in the mines was twelve thousand men. There was just no way Bell Island could compete with Labrador. The ore in the north was not only a better grade product, but it was on top of the ground with only a few feet of topsoil (overburden) covering it. On Bell Island the poorer grade ore was now being mined three miles out under Conception Bay. The cost of bringing this ore to the surface became prohibitive, and layoffs kept coming, until finally, four years after the Smallwood mine opened, DOSCO Mines on Bell Island closed down on June 30, 1966.

Wrapping It Up at the News—We Had a Great Rapport with the Police and Firemen

My last assignment at the *Daily News* was not very exciting, but at least it was a "first." In July, 1964, the new icebreaker *John Cabot* arrived on its maiden voyage and we went to the waterfront to get a shot. This was the first combined cable-repair ship and icebreaker in the world. It was also the first cable ship to be built in Canada. It weighed five thousand tons, was 313 feet long, and carried a crew of eighty-five. Later that month I left the paper, after twenty enjoyable and exciting years. Present-day reporters are sometimes amazed at the freedom of movement we had back in the early years. For instance, at the Hull Home fire of 1948 where thirty-four people lost their lives, I went into the burned-out building and took pictures of firemen searching for bodies. Then at the morgue, I wandered in and photographed bodies lying around on the floor, with relatives trying to identify them. No one ever questioned me. At that time, in the forties, there was no television in Newfoundland, and only two press photographers in St. John's; Albert Young at the *Telegram*, and me at the *Daily News*. The city was much smaller then. We were almost pioneers. Well, certainly Albert Young was. He was the first press photographer in Newfoundland. Both of us were pretty well known in police circles and by the fire department. We had a great rapport with them. Here are two examples: one day at the *News*, we had a report of an oil truck overturned on Topsail Road near Cowan Avenue. When I reached the scene, the truck was on fire and firemen had arrived and were about to turn on their hoses. As I jumped out of my car, camera in hand, I heard one of the firemen say, "Hold it a minute, here comes Kennedy." On another occasion, three men had been found guilty of murdering a woman in St. Phillips, and were at the courthouse being sentenced for their crime. Outside, hundreds of people waited near the Duckworth Street entrance, and the police van was parked there with rear doors open. Policemen stood by, ready for the criminals, waiting for them to exit the building. A plainclothes policeman strolled over and whispered into my ear, "Frank, they're not coming out this way, they're coming out the Water Street door." I said "Thanks," stood there for a few more seconds and casually walked over and down the courthouse steps. Sure enough, there were three unmarked cars lined up on Water Street, with two men in each car. There was not another soul around. I waited only a few minutes before the courthouse door opened, and out came the three convicts, each handcuffed to a policeman. I got a great shot of the six men coming down the long front steps, and we scooped the *Telegram* on that one. The police van on Duckworth Street was just a set-up to fool the crowd. This trio had been convicted of a heinous crime, and the police were afraid they might be attacked as they left the building.

Assignments: The Good and the Sad

Taking the sad ones first, the Hull Home fire (related earlier in this book) was the worst. Another unpleasant one happened, ironically, during "Fire Prevention Week" in 1950, when six people were killed as the result of a fire on Prince's Street in downtown St. John's. I was gotten out of bed at 2:00 a. m. for that one, and our "Stop the press" photo that morning showed firemen working in vain on two of the young victims, trying desperately to revive them. My absolute favorite photo was also taken at the scene of a fire, and I'm sorry no copy exists today. It's somewhere in the *Daily News* files, of course, but I don't remember the year and so was unable to locate it. I was covering a late night fire on Water Street west, where a restaurant was on fire. Suddenly a distraught woman appeared and told firemen her infant child was in a cot on the third floor, and she couldn't get up there because the stairway was on fire. A fireman rushed up a ladder to the third floor, took off his hat and smashed a window, crawled in and disappeared. Hundreds of spectators looked up in horror and many gasped as black smoke began pouring from the opening. In only a few seconds the fireman appeared at the window with a bundle in his arms. It was the child wrapped in a blue blanket. Carefully getting back on the ladder, he descended, holding on with one hand. When he reached the ground, he passed the unharmed infant to the joyous mother, as the spectators gave him a hearty round of applause. That's when I got my favorite news photo. It appeared on page one of the *Daily News* next morning, and clearly showed the fireman at the foot of the ladder, handing the baby to the outstretched arms of the grateful mother. In the background were the spectators with their hands raised applauding the hero. Other memorable assignments were Bob Hope at Pepperell, Louis Armstrong, the well-known American entertainer, and Karsh, the world famous portrait photographer.

Pittsburgh Paint building at rear of Newfoundland Hotel was destroyed in early morning blaze in 1958. Daily News *Photo by Frank Kennedy*

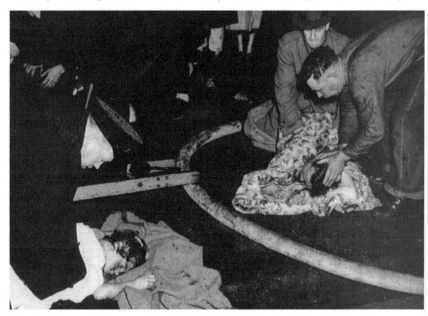

Tragic fire on Princess Street in St. John's during "Fire Prevention Week" in 1950 took six lives. Here firemen try to revive victims. Daily News *Photo by Frank Kennedy*

Bob Hope

For Americans serving at Fort Pepperell, Newfoundland was considered overseas, and as Bob Hope and his troupe entertained virtually everywhere in the world where U. S. troops were stationed, he didn't forget about Newfoundland. Hope came to Pepperell in the late forties, with the orchestra that always accompanied him, Les Brown and his Band of Renown. They put off a great show at the base theater, which was filled to capacity. It had been announced that only one representative of each newspaper would be allowed in, owing to the limited seating space and the great number of servicemen. I wanted to see Bob Hope, and got the okay from my boss, Mr. Currie. Nels Squires, our other photographer, a lover of the "Big Band" sound, and a musician in his own right, was very anxious to see Les Brown and his band, but as I mentioned, only one rep of each newspaper would be allowed to go there. As it happened, each weekend the *Daily News* would gather all the local news stories of that week, and reprint them in a small tabloid-size paper called, *The Observers Weekly*. When Nels and I both turned up at the door of the base theater, each with a press camera, I simply said, "*Daily News*", Nels said, "Observers Weekly," and in we went. It was a terrific show. Bob Hope was a riot, and the band was fantastic. Nels and I agreed no matter how good a stereo, or any other sound system is, you just can't beat being there, seeing and hearing them live!

Louis Armstrong

Louis Armstrong put on a concert at the Memorial Stadium in the sixties, in front of a packed house. He was a star of stage, radio, television and motion pictures, and was well known for mopping his brow with a white handkerchief, while blowing his famous trumpet. Louis held a press conference at the Newfoundland Hotel, and he was a joy to behold. He showed such good humor and a big friendly smile, as he shook hands with us all. There were drinks all round. One of the reporters asked," How come you always seem to be in such a good mood? "Old Satchmo replied," I'm just doin' what comes naturally."

Karsh

Karsh was another matter. This world-renowned portrait photographer from Ottawa charged four figures for a sitting, and was invited to come to Newfoundland to photograph several prominent citizens, including Smallwood, who was not yet premier. Karsh arrived in St. John's in January 1949 and Mr. Currie assigned Jack White and myself to do a story on him. Naturally I was a bit apprehensive going to meet the man at the Newfoundland Hotel, but I was anxious to see him, nevertheless. This was the classic portrait artist of the camera, who had photographed kings and queens, world leaders, statesmen, great artists and literary geniuses. This was the man who had plucked the cigar from the mouth of Sir Winston Churchill, and captured his look of belligerence, in a photograph that became one of the most widely reproduced photos in the history of photography. And I was about to photograph him! The whole idea was thrilling, but a greater thrill was yet to come.

At the hotel, Yousuf Karsh welcomed us into his suite, and with his delightful Armenian accent, told us how much he enjoyed visiting beautiful Newfoundland. As Jack White sat and interviewed him, without asking his permission I grabbed a few candid shots. When White was finished, I began to apologize, saying, "I hope you didn't mind my taking candid shots while you were being interviewed. " "Not at all," he replied, "In fact, I must compliment you on your technique."That made my day.

Ron Pumphrey to the Rescue

In the mid-1950s when Bell Island mines were in full operation, DOSCO (the mining company) had put new mining equipment in use underground, and wanted photos of this machinery at work. They hired the *Daily News* photographer (me) to do the job. The work was going on three miles down from the mine entrance, and two miles out under the ocean. Ore cars ran on tracks down the three miles on a fairly steep slope, and were pulled back filled with ore. To get the workmen down there, a special slow trip was made, with the men sitting in the ore cars. I had to be there at 8:00 a. m. to make this trip, as there was no other way of getting down until 4:00p.m. When I went to Portugal Cove that morning to take the 7:00 a. m. crossing, the ferry was already filled with cars and trucks, with no room for my car. I grabbed my gadget bag of flashbulbs, the big press camera and walked aboard. Once on the island I would get a taxi to the mine head. To my horror, I discovered I had left my film packs in the car in Portugal Cove. When we docked at 7:20 a. m., I was almost in a panic. I knew the stores on the island wouldn't have this size film (4x5 packs) even if any were open this early. Then it occurred to me that Ron Pumphrey lived here. He had a press camera, as he worked for the *Evening Telegram*. Maybe he would loan me some film. Where did he live? I asked the taxi driver if he knew. To my great relief, he replied, "Oh yes, everyone knows where Ron lives, I'll take you there."

When we got to Ron's house, I explained my problem, and he showed me his press camera. Oh God! It was a different size. Ron told me not to worry, he had lots of film and would lend me his camera for the day as well. I never forgot that goodwill gesture; I'd only met Ron a few times on news stories, and we were really not friends, at that time, he working for the opposition paper and all. Thanks to Ron, I made the 8:00 a. m. slow run down into the mine, got the job done, and came back up at four o'clock. I returned the camera, and next day replaced the film. Thanks Ron. Good man!

On another occasion, Nels Squires and I were down in the mines for a day doing a story, and our mining company guide was a man named Frank Squires. There were hundreds of miners working in various locations, of course, and it was funny, but every time someone would say, "Hello, Frank," I would look around, and every time one of the miners said, "Hello Mr. Squires" Nels would look around.

Frank Kennedy at the controls of an iron ore train, two miles out under Conception Bay. *Photo by Nels Squires.*

Jack A. White

One of the best reporters at the "*News*" in my time was Jack A. White, later to become a magistrate. As well as writing for the *News* he was for a number of years the Newfoundland reporter for *Time Magazine*, and often had stories published there, sometimes with my photographs. I mentioned earlier, how I was once nearly fired from the *News* (the "Twilight in Yachau" incident). Sometime later Jack nearly lost his job for embarrassing the publisher, Honorable John S. Currie, Chancey's father. This is how it happened: the M.C.L.I. (Methodist College Literary Institute) were having a special speech night, and Jack was told to cover it. Honorable John Currie would be one of the speakers, and he gave Jack a copy of his speech in advance, together with the names of the other speakers. It so happened that Jack A. had a very important date that night that he didn't want to miss. Jack was a clever guy. During the day he contacted all the other speakers and got copies of their speeches as well. Now he was all set. Early in the evening Jack went to the MCLI auditorium, before the meeting started, and made sure he was seen by Mr. Currie. Then he mingled with the crowd and slipped out the door. Jack kept his date as planned, and came back to the office after midnight and wrote the story. He condensed what the various speakers had said, including the comments of Honorable. J. S. Currie, who had said this, that, and the other thing. Jack typed up the story and went home. When he came in the next afternoon, reporter Gordon Barron said," J. S. wants to see you. "Very good, thought Jack, he probably wants to compliment me on my story. But Barron added," He seems pretty upset."

Jack A. went upstairs and into Currie's office and J. S. glared at him. "Well," he said, "You made a fine mess of that story this morning. I was never so embarrassed in my whole life!" "What was wrong with it, sir?" asked Jack. The angry boss replied, "Well, obviously you didn't stay for the whole meeting last night, because the emcee forgot to introduce me, and I didn't speak at all! "

Surprising Bank Note Trivia

A few decades ago, when the present Canadian bank notes were being introduced, the royal mint sent an agent to various newspapers across the country, to show samples of the new currency. When that man visited the *Daily News* and displayed the new bills, Mr. Currie, our boss, thought that John O'Brien and myself, being photo-engravers as well as photographers, would be interested in examining them. He called us to his office and introduced the mint man, who proudly showed us the new bank notes. I happened to have our engravers' glass in my pocket, a powerful magnifying glass similar to the eye piece used by jewelers. I closely inspected the fine detail on a twenty-dollar note, and then, passing it and the glass to John O'Brien, quipped "Well, John, we're going to have a hard job reproducing these. "For a moment there was a look of horror on the mint man's face until he realized I was joking, then we all laughed. We, or anyone else for that matter, certainly would have a job reproducing these new notes. They had no less than five colors, and this was long before the sophisticated color copiers had been invented. And by the way, most of these new machines today, have a chip built in, that prevents them from copying currency.

Oh yes! Here is the surprising trivia: take a look at the back of a five dollar note, if you will. How many fives are there, not counting the serial number? Two, you say. Correct! Now please look at the front. How many fives are there? Two, you say again. Wrong. As Joey Smallwood would say, "Not two, not five, not twenty-five, not fifty-five, not five hundred, but five thousand!" More, in fact, as I stopped counting at five thousand. (My former boss, Ralph Balodis once told me I had great patience.) Anyway, yes, I counted them, and when I got to five thousand, I gave up. These wavy blue and orange and yellow and green lines are actually rows of tiny fives. Yes, more than five thousand. Even the sky over the parliament buildings is nothing but a repetition of "5 BANK OF CANADA 5 BANQUE DU CANADA 5" and the background of the large word, "Canada "is the same. So much for useless trivia.

While five colors are used on these notes, I will never understand why the United States bank notes are still printed in just two colors, black on the front, and green on the back. Any half-ass engraver with mediocre equipment could turn out counterfeits of these by the thousands—and probably does!

The Case of the Missing Accident Victim

About 2:00 a. m. one morning as I was driving up Water Street west after work, I was surprised to see a car coming in the opposite direction, and then crashing into the rear of a parked car. The impact was so violent, that the rear of the moving car lifted five feet off the ground. I pulled over and jumped out of my car and went back to the accident scene. The driver's door was open and he was hanging out on the ground, with his legs still in the car. He was unconscious with blood streaming from his forehead. Kneeling beside him was a man shouting, "He's dying! He's dying!" I said I'd call an ambulance. Nearby, I noticed a man looking out from his doorway. I went to him and asked him to make the call. Then I drove back to the *News* office on Duckworth Street to get my camera. As I arrived there, the ambulance raced by. Picking up the camera and some flash bulbs, I drove back to the scene as fast as I could, hoping to get a shot of the victim being placed in the ambulance. When I got out of my car, the attendants were looking around for the victim. By now a dozen spectators were there, but no sign of anyone needing help. The ambulance driver demanded, "Who called us?" I said I did, and that there was a man lying unconscious on the ground five minutes ago. He looked at me very skeptically. "Well, where the heck is he now?" he asked. I couldn't answer. Just then the police arrived and soon discovered that the accident victim lived nearby, and his friends had carried him into his house. He was drunk, and although bleeding profusely, he was not seriously injured. He had only a gash on the forehead. The police wanted to go in and see him, but the relatives would not allow them inside the house. Obviously, they didn't want the cops to discover his condition, and after all, according to the law, he had twenty-four hours in which to report his accident. While the ambulance driver went back empty-handed, I did not. That morning, at least we had a picture of the wrecked car on page one.

Lunch with John C. Doyle: Fugitive from Justice

Millionaire businessman John C. Doyle held concessions for much of western Labrador in the early 60s, and when the mining companies moved in and started producing iron ore, he was paid royalties for every ton they brought out. Doyle contacted Chancey Currie at the *News,* requesting two pages of pictures on the iron ore development and suggesting to get together and sort out some photographs. Currie agreed but said Frank

Kennedy should come along, as he was the person who usually laid out pages of photographs. Next day I found myself sitting in the dining room at the Newfoundland Hotel with Doyle and my boss. I found Doyle to be a refined gentleman, charming and cultured and not the least bit patronizing. After a fine lunch we went to his suite where he produced about fifty pictures of various phases of mining. Doyle and Currie then sat back and chatted as I went through the photographs, picking out about twenty of the best shots. I arranged these into a two-page format and asked the two gentlemen what they thought of the layout. Doyle seemed quite pleased, and of course, so was Mr. Currie.

In his book *No Holds Barred*, John Crosbie describes John C. Doyle as not only charming, personable, brilliant and cultured, but also an evil genius. He says a lot of other nasty things about Doyle as well, which I won't repeat here, just in case Doyle should ever return to Newfoundland. Nevertheless, there was certainly some merit in Crosbie's evaluation. When Doyle first came to this province from Chicago in the mid-1950s, he wined and dined Premier Smallwood, took him on trips abroad, and then took advantage of the friendship that had developed. Smallwood let Doyle's company, Canadian Javelin, have the concessions to the mineral rights in western Labrador. And that was only the beginning. Smallwood desperately wanted to start a third paper mill in Newfoundland, and use some of the hundreds of square miles of timber in Labrador to feed it. Doyle persuaded him that a liner board mill would be better, and that Stephenville would be the best place to put it. Joey gave Doyle a guarantee of $53 million to build it. That was the price Doyle said it would cost. Construction started in 1967, but in four years the job was not even half finished and all the money was gone. Secret loans were then made by the provincial government, through Smallwood, amounting to another $24 million, without the approval or knowledge of the members of the House or the cabinet. Much of this money was funneled into Doyle-owned companies for undisclosed services. Some even went for lavish furniture for Doyle's luxury apartment. Smallwood's Liberal government was finally defeated in the fall election of 1971, but before leaving office, Smallwood guaranteed another $30 million loan to Javelin without any agreement as to what the money was to be used for. When Frank Moores' Conservative government took over in January 1972, they had a huge multi-million dollar unfinished white elephant on their hands. With so much money already gone into it, they just had to spend a few more millions to complete the job, and the final cost was nearly $160 million. The mill never did operate in the black, but at least it kept a lot of people employed. The cost of bringing wood from Labrador was too high and there was no steady supply available on the island. By 1979, the loss of $100 for each ton of liner board produced, could not be sustained and so the plant was forced to close. Later, all the assets were transferred to Abitibi-Price who converted the mill to paper making. And so another of Joey's dreams materialized, but not in his time.

In the meantime, John C. Doyle had been arrested in 1973 in Montreal, on a variety of charges of fraud and stock manipulation. He spent a night in jail and was released on $75,000 bail. This was only peanuts for him, of course, so he skipped out and went to Panama, just south of Mexico. The Republic of Panama does not have a treaty regarding extradition with Canada or the United States, and at this writing, Doyle, now in his eighties, is living in his penthouse there, but is still on the wanted list in both countries.

1964: From Newspaper to Television—From Stills to Movies

At age sixteen I bought my first camera, a Baby Brownie, for $1. 20, and developed my own films in a walk-in closet in my mother's home on Patrick Street. Photography was my hobby for the first few working years after leaving school, and when I joined the *Daily News* in 1944, I was now being paid for my hobby. It was great! During the last few years at the *News*, I took up movie making as a hobby, and hoped that some day I would become a professional motion-picture cameraman. When CBC, after years of trying, finally got permission to operate a TV station from St. John's in 1964, I was hired as just that. So, here we go again: paid for my hobby for another twenty-two years, and given the best equipment to work with as well! While at the News I made movies of weddings and other celebrations and was once asked to make a documentary of the Children's Rehabilitation Centre. I did this, and the film was sent to the CBC radio studio to have a sound track added. The film was then aired on CJON-TV, which at that time was the only television station in the city. A year later when the CBC did get their license, they wanted another motion-picture cameraman. John O'Brien was already with them, having left the *News* two years earlier. He had an office in the radio building, and whenever mainland CBC wanted some Newfoundland footage, he would shoot it. I applied for this second cameraman's position, along with ten other people, and was called in for an interview with the director, Bill Galgay and Joan Kelland, his assistant. They told me they had seen my Rehabilitation Centre film the previous year, and were impressed with it, and asked me when could I start with them. This was July 3, and I said I wanted to give the *News* some notice, and agreed to start a month later, which I did. Little did I know that my first assignment would be a cowboy picture, starring among others, Joey Smallwood!

A Wild West Start at the CBC: The Flying L Ranch

Harold Lees, a cattle rancher from western Canada, was interested in starting a large ranch on the Burin Peninsula, and had been in that area as early as 1960 looking over the territory. He found a lot of bogland there, but felt that much of this could be drained and turned into fine pasture land, for perhaps as many as five thousand head of cattle. Although he raised his animals in Saskatchewan, most of his beef was shipped to Europe, and the Burin Peninsula was 2500 miles closer than his ranch. This would cut down the shipping costs considerably. In the fall of 1963 he formed a company, The Flying L Ranch Company Limited, and brought in one hundred and twenty-five animals on a trial basis. He figured they should easily survive the Newfoundland winter, which was much milder than Saskatchewan. He was right. The cattle had no problem living through the winter, and this was great encouragement, along with Premier Smallwood's promise to grant him several hundred square miles of rangeland, including twenty square miles for a ranch near Winterland, just west of Marystown. In early August 1964, trainloads of bulls and cows began arriving at Goobies, near the top of the peninsula, and by August 25, nine hundred animals were grazing there, waiting for their next move to greener pastures. They were to be driven down ninety miles to the new ranch, "The Flying L," and this was my first assignment, covering that cattle drive.

Producer Rab Carnell, sound man Bill Murphy and myself went to Swift Current, fifteen miles from Goobies, the day before the round-up, and stayed overnight at Beck's Cabins. Rab had phoned ahead and reserved a cabin for three, but when we got there, we found one of the three single beds had two legs broken off, and this was the only cabin available that night. Rab complained to the manager, who came into the cabin and said, "No problem, I'll fix that." Then he took a large metal garbage can, lifted up the bed and placed the can underneath. "There!" he said, and walked out. Bill Murphy asked, "Who's going to sleep on that one? The boss, I suppose." Rab wanted to be fair about it, and decided we'd draw straws. Rab had been with CBC radio for a number of years, and when he drew the short straw, he declared, "Well damn it, after all these years with the CBC, I've got to sleep on a garbage can!" Next morning we were up early, and so were the cowboys. They began the roundup by circling the scattered herd on horseback, and funneling them towards the Burin Peninsula highway.

Premier Smallwood rode the range in fine style, on a fine brown mare, and really looked the part with his cowboy suit, boots, red neckerchief and ten-gallon hat (oops, forty-five litre). Horseback riding was nothing new for Joey, of course, as he had several riding horses on his own ranch on Roache's Line, and this was probably one of them. Riding with Joey, side by side, were the two head "honchos" of the new company, Harold Lees and Art Hall, both from out west. Much of the area along the highway was fenced, and there was very little trouble keeping the 900 animals on the straight and narrow. However, in other sections, the road ran through barrens and bogs, and often some cows would wander onto these, and it was great getting shots of the wranglers doing their stuff, getting the animals back in line. Our crew of three became separated during the morning, and after a couple of hours, Rab Carnell asked Bill Murphy if he'd seen Kennedy. Bill said, "Well, the last time I saw him he was down the road standing in front of a big bull and getting a close-up of his horns." He may have been exaggerating somewhat, but we did get some interesting shots. The herd was being driven rather slowly; Lee didn't want his animals to lose too much fat on their long trek, and this was fine with us. We were able to walk along with them and get ample footage. For one shot I stood with the camera rolling, as hundreds of cows passed by on a fairly narrow section of road. Then into the view finder came this big bull astride a cow, copulating as the whole group moved along. That shot is now in the blooper tape at CBNT. Joey rode along for the first ten miles, until the cowboys stopped for a chuck wagon dinner. During that western style meal, he told us he took part in the drive to show the government's support for the venture. He felt this was the start of another thriving new industry for Newfoundland. The film we made was shown across the country on the national program, "Country Canada," and was also used on the first "Land and Sea" program, when we initially went on the air from St. John's in October of that year.

The addition of the nine hundred head of cattle at the Flying L now made a total of over a thousand animals on the range on the boot of the peninsula. During the fall and winter, young boys were thrilled to see real cowboys rounding up doggies (stray calves) in their towns. After the first year, however, the government began getting complaints from town councils. They said the roaming cattle were contaminating their water supplies, and that picnic sites and swimming areas were being polluted. A Grand Bank butcher said Lees was allowing some cows to starve to death, and he had seen more than a dozen dead animals on the range. Lee countered by saying some residents were shoot-

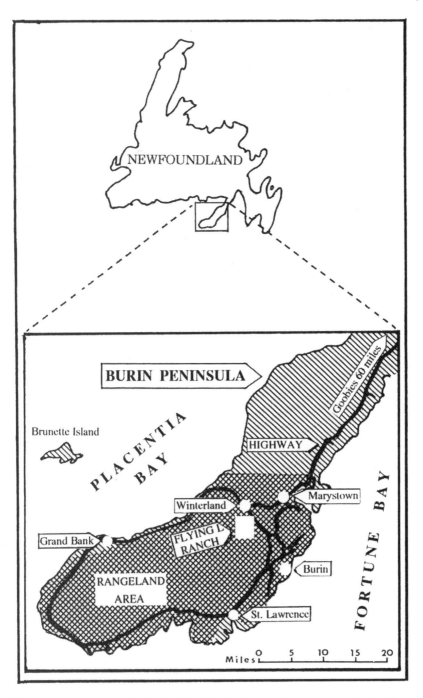

Map shows how nearly half of the Burin Peninsula was granted to the Flying L Ranch for rangeland in 1964.

ing the cows for sport, and others were actually rustling the cattle. He discovered that bog-reclamation was much more expensive than he had anticipated, and subsidies from the government were not as ample as he hoped. He had to borrow money from the bank to bring in feed, and for salaries for the cow hands. In two years the Flying L Ranch was in big financial trouble. None of the loans were being repaid, so the bank decided to foreclose. In the spring of 1966, the Toronto Dominion Bank took possession of the cattle, in lieu of payment of more than half a million dollars then owing. The bank auctioned the animals for an undisclosed amount. Many of the animals were never found. Some had fallen over cliffs, others were lost in the bogs. Still others may still be roaming the hundreds of square miles of rangeland. Another of Joey's new industries had bitten the dust. In any case, if you happen to be hunting moose on the Burin Peninsula, be very careful before you pull the trigger. You might be aiming at the last bull of the Flying L.

Return To Gallipoli in 1965: Forgive But Remember—Fifty Years Later

On September 22, 1915, Private Walter McWhirter of Humbermouth became the first Newfoundlander to be killed in action in the First World War. He was one of forty-six Newfoundlanders to die and be buried in Gallipoli, Turkey, and fifty years later, some of their comrades went back and laid wreaths on their graves. The return to Gallipoli came about when the government of Turkey invited the three hundred and fifty Australian and New Zealand war veterans still living to come back for celebrations marking the 50th anniversary of the invasion of that peninsula. They even sent a twelve thousand ton ocean liner to pick them up. They wanted to meet their former foes on a friendly basis, and allow them to visit the graves of their fallen comrades.

Premier Smallwood contacted CBC Director Bill Galgay, to say that he was going over with seven surviving Newfoundland

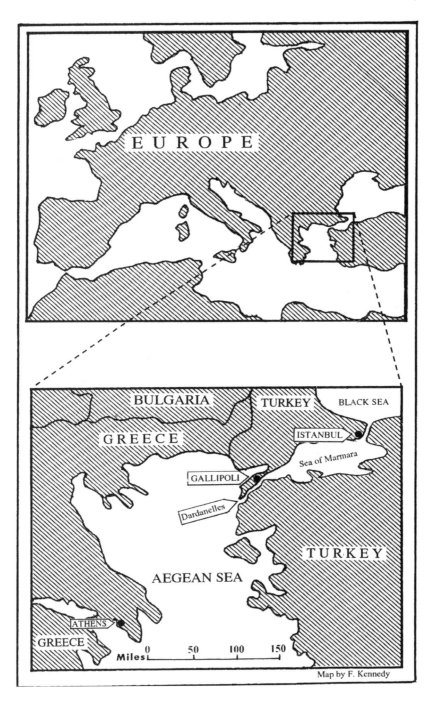

Map shows location of Gallipoli in south-eastern Europe.

veterans, and suggested he send a camera crew to cover the momentous occasion. Galgay thought it was such a good idea, that he not only sent a four-man crew, but went along himself to "look after the boys." The Newfoundland veterans were Lieutenant Colonel B. Butler, D. S. O. of Corner Brook; Captain George Hicks, M. C. of Grand Falls; Sergeant C. Parsons, M. M. & Bar of St. John's; W. R. Martin, St. John's; Albert Delaney, St. George's; George Harsant of St. John's; and Lieutenant Bernard Forsey, then living in California. They were all willing to forgive their former foes and remember their fallen comrades. This Newfoundland delegation flew to London, England, and stayed a week before going to Gallipoli, and was accompanied by former lieutenant governor Sir Leonard Outerbridge, D. S. O., Honorary Colonel of the Royal Newfoundland Regiment; Honorable Myles Murray, Vice chairman of the Royal Canadian Legion and Colonel Jos. O'Driscoll. We met the Newfoundlanders in London, where we stayed overnight, and next morning boarded a BOAC Comet Jet with them for the flight to Istanbul, Turkey. The plane touched down in Paris for half an hour, just long enough for us to dart out to a souvenir shop and buy a tiny Eiffel tower. In Istanbul the Newfoundlanders checked in to the four-star Istanbul Hilton Hotel, where the veterans found accommodations much better than when they last left Turkey fifty years earlier.

Conditions then were absolutely horrible. The trenches where they stayed were filthy, with knee-deep mud. Diseases were rampant; more than half of the thousand Newfoundlanders fighting there came down with typhoid and dysentery, and in November when the mud froze, many of the soldiers suffered frozen feet and gangrene, resulting in many amputations. To add insult to injury, the Allies lost the battle! The terrible eight-month engagement was the result of Turkey entering the war on the side of Germany. Russia was on our side and their warships were in the Black Sea. In order for these ships to get to Western Europe to help the Allies, they would have to sail through the Dardanelles, a narrow Turkish channel, forty miles long. There was no way they could do that with enemy fortifications on both sides of the channel. Sir Winston Churchill, first lord of the admiralty,

The *S.S. Karadenize* took the Newfoundland veterans on the five-hundred mile cruise from Istanbul to Gallipoli and then to Athens in 1965. *Photo by Frank Kennedy*

The Newfoundland delegation at Azmak Cemetary. Recumbent placques were used in most cemetaries rather than the usual upright headstones which sometimes tend to topple. *Photo by Frank Kennedy*

contrived the idea of invading the Gallipoli Peninsula, going overland, and capturing the capital, Istanbul, thus knocking Turkey out of the war. Unfortunately it didn't work, but many lives were lost in the attempt.

The invasion began in April 1915, when thousands of allied troops, mostly Australians and New Zealanders, (ANZACS), swarmed ashore and were met by heavy artillery fire from the surrounding hills. The Allies dug in but made little headway for the entire summer. On September 20, the Newfoundland Regiment went ashore at Suvla Bay to join them. The first five hundred and the second five hundred to go overseas went there. They had been trained in Scotland, and this would be their first engagement with the enemy. Within hours fifteen soldiers were wounded, as they dug fox holes and trenches to protect themselves. Two days later Private McWhirter was hit by a shell and, as mentioned, became the first Newfoundlander killed in action in that great war. The next day, Private William Hardy of St. John's was killed by a sniper bullet. In two weeks, however, the regiment had moved to the front line, and were now in trenches less than 200 feet from the Turks.

Sporadic rifle fire was picking off allied soldiers from a nest of snipers on a nearby hill, but three Newfoundland soldiers attacked and wiped them out. Later they received the regiment's first awards for bravery. Private Richard Hynes and Sergeant Greene were awarded the distinguished Conduct Medal, and Lieutenant Donnelly the Military Cross. Things were going pretty good now for the Newfoundland Regiment soldiers, and they wondered why they couldn't charge forward and defeat the Turks. They didn't realize that the enemy fortifications on the hills of Gallipoli were invincible. By November, thousands of troops had been killed on the beaches, and another enemy, winter, had to be dealt with. There was little shelter in the fox holes and trenches and hundreds of soldiers suffered severe frostbite. The hardships were insurmountable, and the decision was taken to pull out. The Newfoundland Regiment was the last to leave, and those who had died were buried right there on the beaches, and later transferred to cemeteries on the Gallipoli Peninsula.

Although they lost that battle, the Allies won the war. In this fierce struggle, the Allies wore down the Turkish army to such an extent that they were later defeated in Palestine, thus hastening the end of the war. The Regiment later moved on to France, where hundreds laid down their lives in the infamous July Drive at Beaumont Hamel.

Back at the Hilton Hotel, the Newfoundland veterans had to wait a day for the Australians to arrive from "down under," and two more days for them to sail. They spent much of the three days taking in the sights. So did we. On the first day the CBC crew did a lot of walking, led by Mr. Galgay. Also with us were Dick O'Brien, Dave Gunn and Harvey Morgan. When we got back to the hotel in the early evening we were quite hungry and looking forward to a good meal there. I said to Mr. Galgay, "Shall we meet in the dining room in fifteen minutes?" He said, "No. Meet me in the lobby. We'll go and look for an Italian restaurant." Fifteen minutes later we were walking again, hungrier than ever. Every few minutes one of us would point to a restaurant and say hopefully, "There's one." Galgay would say, "No. It's not Italian." Finally he found one and we were thankful. The menu was written in Turkish or Italian; it was Dutch to us, so we ordered the same as Galgay. At least the meal was filling, if a trifle spicy, and then the waiter presented the dessert menu. Again most of us followed the chief's choice, but one of us recognized the word "orange" in one of the selections, and ordered that. What a disappointment when he was passed an ordinary unpeeled orange on a plate with a knife and fork!

Joey Shows Us Around

On the second day we met Premier Smallwood in the spacious lobby and he asked Mr. Galgay if he had shown us around. Galgay assured him he had. Joey asked, "Did you see the Blue Mosque?" Galgay said, "No" "Did you see the Covered Market?" "No" "Did you see Saint Sophie Museum?" "No." "Well," said Smallwood, "You haven't seen very much. Let me show you

Utility farm cart with Smallwood and the Newfoundland veterans stuck in the mud on the way to the remote Azmak cemetary. *Photo by Frank Kennedy*

Farm tractor pulls empty cart out of the mud. *Photo by Frank Kennedy.*

around. I've been here five times already. And besides, you'll need long rubbers to get in to the cemeteries. I'll show you where to buy them. Let's get a taxi." Then looking around at the rest of us, he asked, "How many of you are there?" Galgay replied, "Five." Smallwood said, "Let's get two taxis" He gave us the grand tour of Istanbul. First we visited the Saint Sophia Museum. It's the fourth largest place of worship in the world. It is actually a huge mosque, 321 feet long with a dome 182 feet high. The Anglican Cathedral in St. John's could easily fit inside, with room to spare. The building is over fourteen hundred years old, and has survived numerous earthquakes and several fires. We had to take off our shoes and put on supplied slippers before being allowed to walk in. Next we went to the Blue Mosque, equally impressive, and then on to the Covered Market, an unusual arrangement of small shops with a roof over the whole block. Here Joey brought us to a footwear store where we purchased the knee rubbers he said we would need. Only four moderately priced pairs remained, so I had to take a very expensive pair. Joey talked the proprietor into giving them to me at the same price as the others. He said that seeing as to how he had brought in five new customers, he should at least give one of them some discount. I thanked both of them.

The twelve thousand ton ocean liner, *Karadeniz*, sailed from Istanbul at midnight on Friday, April 23, 1965, with all the veterans on board: Australians, New Zealanders (ANZACS) and the Newfoundlanders. Sailing all day Saturday along the very calm Sea of Marmara, and into the Dardanelles, the ship arrived in Gallipoli at ten o'clock Sunday morning. I was one of the first off the ship. I wanted to get what I felt was the most important shot of the whole show: the Newfoundland veterans setting foot on Gallipoli, fifty years later. Mr. Galgay was not far behind me. He walked up behind a big shed, then came back and told me excitedly that the Turks were up there dressed as they were fifty years ago. He told me to come up and take their pictures. I said, "But, sir, I want to get the Newfoundlanders coming off the ship first" Mr. Galgay was an expert at radio and electronics, but knew practically nothing about television, and what he said nearly floored me. He ordered, "Never mind them, you'll have lots of time to take their pictures later!" You didn't argue with W. F. Galgay. Up I went with him and took a quick shot of the colorful Turks, then rushed back in time to get the shot I really needed. When our veterans met the Turkish veterans, it was wonderful to see and photograph the smiling faces, the handshakes and the hugs. It was a genuine display of mutual friendship and forgiveness. Even during the war, the Turkish soldiers had openly admired the bravery and courage of the Newfoundland soldiers, and here today, a Turkish Guard of Honor saluted them. The intermingling of the hundreds of Allied and Turkish veterans presented a scene of organized confusion, and the handshaking and back-slapping was a joy to behold.

After ceremonies on the waterfront, chartered buses took the veterans to the battlefields on the shores of Suvla Bay. What they saw there was much different from what they left behind fifty years earlier. The outlines of the trenches were still there, but now overgrown with scrub. The mud was gone, the filth was gone, the frost was gone and the snipers were gone, but the memories lingered on. The old soldiers walked around, pointing here and there, recounting some of their harrowing experiences. On Monday the Newfoundland delegation went to the cemeteries where the Newfoundlanders were buried. A bus went as far inland as possible, but the last three miles were boggy and muddy and impassable even for a four-wheel drive. Turkish officials who accompanied us had arranged two wooden carts with seats, to be pulled along by farm tractors, and this is how the final leg was traversed. Even then sometimes they would get stuck, and all hands would have to get out so that the empty carts could be pulled free. This was when we needed the long rubbers, Joey knew. At the Green Hill Cemetery, Smallwood laid a wreath on the graves of two unknown Newfoundland soldiers buried there, on behalf of the people of the province. The temperature was a pleasant 75 degrees (24 degrees C.). Most of the Newfoundlanders who died lay in the Azmak Cemetery. This was in a remote area, and the hardest to reach. Our veterans laid wreaths and flowers of remembrance there. The cemeteries there

Premier Smallwood at the entrance to Saint Sophie Museum in Turkey. Left to right: Frank Kennedy, Bill Galgay, Smallwood, Turkish guide and Harvey Morgan. *Photo by Dave Gunn*

Cameraman Kennedy, in front of the "Cross of Sacrifice" monument, films the Newfoundland veterans visiting the graves of their fallen comrades ina cemetery in Turkey. *Photo by Dave Gunn.*

were strikingly beautiful, if disconsolate, with neat rows of small headstones set in well-kept lawns with a variety of colorful flowers and tall trees. All have a common theme, with a massive white stone monument and cross as the centerpiece. The immortal words, "Their name liveth for evermore" are carved on an altar which forms part of the memorial. There are thirty-one allied veterans' cemeteries on the Gallipoli Peninsula, containing the remains of nearly thirty-six thousand brave men who died in the cause of freedom. All these graveyards were built and are well maintained by the Commonwealth Graves Commission, and funded by the various allied nations who are represented there.

The *Karadeniz* housed the veterans for two days while it was tied up in Gallipoli, before sailing 250 miles across the Aegean Sea to Athens, Greece. There the Newfoundlanders did more touring, visiting such attractions as the twenty five hundred-year-old Parthenon, (still in a bad state of disrepair) and the huge sixty-eight thousand seat, all marble stadium, where the original olympic games were held hundreds of years before the coming of Christ. Only men were permitted to take part in the Olympics in the early days. They were mostly chariot races, and women were not even allowed to view the contests. But that's another story. After a day in Athens, the Newfoundland delegation flew home. On board the ship, on the way to Athens, the veterans told us they enjoyed the experience immensely. They had often thought of their friends buried in this far away land, but it never occurred to them that some day they might be privileged to visit their graves, and they were glad they were spared to see that day. Their philosophy is summed up in the words of British Field-Marshal Viscount Slim, K. G. :

"Never believe their lives were wasted. It is not how long a man lives that matters, but what he does with the years that are granted to him. In their short span these men did much. The thought of them should make us and those who are coming after us determined to create, in the years of freedom they gained for us, something that is worthy of their sacrifice."

Official Opening Trans-Canada Highway 1966—Prime Minister Pearson Not Impressed

For three years the Newfoundland government's slogan was, "We'll Finish The Drive In Sixty-Five," and they did just that and officially opened the Trans-Canada Highway (T.C.H.) on July 12, 1966. It had taken sixteen years and $250 million to build the 566 miles of paved highway, and Premier Smallwood ordered a three-day celebration to honor it. Prime Minister Lester Pearson unveiled a plaque in central Newfoundland, and declared the new highway now open to traffic. A giant cavalcade, 2 miles long, started at mile zero near Confederation Building in St. John's a day earlier, and proceeded west to the halfway point just east of Grand Falls, with Tourism Minister Al Vardy in charge. More than one hundred vehicles took part in the parade, and various stops were made at settlements along the way so that residents could view the many impressive floats. The first float carried live actors in make-up and dress, portraying the first inhabitants and travelers in Newfoundland, the Beothuk Indians, complete with their wigwams and canoes. Then came more live actors representing the first white man to walk across the island, W. E. Cormack, and his Indian guide. They had taken fifty-eight days. The next float had a large model of an early steam locomotive, on a giant trailer, representing the first mechanical vehicle to cross Newfoundland after the Reid Newfoundland Company built the railway around the turn of the century. This model had smoke billowing from the stack, and appropriate sound effects. Then came the four-wheel-drive Land Rover used by Smallwood and Greg Power in 1958, to be the first to drive across the island.

Smallwood, of course, was in the first limousine, followed by cars carrying cabinet ministers and other VIPs, including Transport Minister Jack Pickersgill, and preceded by an escort of the R. C. M. P. Several large construction trucks took part, as well as ten media cars, including ours. With so many stops, it took three days to reach Port-aux-Basques, but as planned, at the halfway mark ten miles east of Grand Falls, a crowd of 2000 gathered to see Prime Minister Lester Pearson unveil the plaque and declare the last link of the Trans-Canada Highway now officially open. The plaque is mounted on the front of a sixty foot tall column of native granite three hundred yards from the road. In honor of the prime minister that huge cairn is called "Pearson's Peak." The Prime Minister received a great round of applause at the unveiling and seemed happy to participate in the ceremonies until Smallwood spoke over the public address system. Smallwood addressed his remarks directly to Pearson. He said "We are going to build a road across Labrador and a tunnel under the straits of Bell Isle, but we need some help to do that. Not men, we have the men, but we need a little cash, say, $60 or $70 million, or $70 or $80 million, or maybe $100 million dollars." Looking straight at Pearson, he continued, "If you will pay us ninety cents for each dollar spent to build this tunnel and road, then Canada will be a mighty nation and Newfoundland a mighty province." When Pearson took the microphone he said he was glad to come and open the highway, but he now realized the real reason the premier had invited him was to see about the future. He acknowledged the appreciation of the people, but was not impressed with Smallwood asking him for money in front of thousands of people, not to mention the media. Nevertheless, he said he would give the request sympathetic consideration. Several other government officials spoke on the advantages of this new highway, before the playing of "Oh Canada" ended the ceremony. The cavalcade moved on to Corner Brook for the night, then on to Port-aux-Basques the following morning, to end the three day celebration.

First Road Cruiser Trip

Two years after the opening, the first Canadian National (C.N.) Road Cruiser made the trip across the island on November 20, 1968. This bus carried no paying passengers, just government and C. N. officials and media people. The CBC sent me with my movie camera to cover that first trip, and I was quite pleased with the cooperation I received from the driver and other C. N. officials.

Having taken an "establishing shot," of the railway station and a close-up of the cruiser parked nearby, I shot footage of the passengers entering the bus. I asked the driver to drive away from the station without me, so that I could photograph the departure, and then wait a few hundred feet up the road for me to get on board. Once or twice on a particularly picturesque section of the highway, the driver would let me out and get footage of the bus passing by in a beautiful setting. Again he would stop and wait for me. Nearly all the seats were filled and everyone seemed to be enjoying the ride. There was a feeling of conviviality all round. Spontaneous singing would break out, and many jokes were told, even some new ones. The excursion was like a paid holiday for most of us. At one point, I'm told, someone suggested to the driver that he go on and leave Kennedy behind! I'm glad that was not from one of the C. N. officials. In Gander the bus stopped for half an hour at a restaurant where we had lunch. There again the driver stopped some distance from the restaurant and allowed me to film the bus arriving. As we were driving by the beautiful Humber River, the bus driver called out, "Mr. Frank Kennedy is wanted on the phone." It was the CBC newsroom in St. John's wanting to know if I had enough footage. When I said I did, they suggested I get off at Corner Brook and fly back. This was a pleasant development. Although I enjoyed the trip out, I was not really looking forward to the long run back the next day, so I did that and we had the story on the news the next night.

Our Pioneering Trip Across in 1955—No Reservations

Although Smallwood and Greg Power were the first to actually drive across the island in 1958, it was possible to drive across as early as 1954, if you were prepared to put your car on a train from Clarenville to Gander, and on a raft to cross the Exploits River. My wife and I made that journey in August 1955. In order to put our car on the train, we had to be at the Clarenville railway station at 9:00 a. m., so we drove to that town on a mostly unpaved road the day before. We stayed the night at the Balmoral

Hotel, where Harry Drover was owner and manager. I knew Harry back in the early 40s when I worked as an office boy at Clancy & Company in St. John's. Harry was a teller at the Royal Bank of Canada on Water Street and was well known for using his gun as a paper weight. True! Every week day I would bring the company's deposit to the bank, and was usually "served" by Harry Drover. He was one of three tellers in brass metal cages, about six by eight feet, with a glass front and a small opening through which business was conducted.

In those days all bank tellers in St. John's had hand guns. Most of these weapons were kept in cash drawers or at least out of sight. But not Harry's! I often marveled at how nonchalantly he would put the loaded revolver on a pile of deposit slips or other documents on the counter in front of him. There were no attempted hold-ups at that bank, I can tell you. But I digress.

After breakfast we drove to the station where the motor cars were being driven onto railway flatcars, two on each flatcar. They were secured by blocks of wood nailed down in front of and behind the auto's wheels. On this day there were more than thirty cars, and the loading took three hours. The train had two passenger coaches and this is where the occupants of the cars rode the 80 miles (128 km) to Gander. The distance on the T. C. H. would be nearly 25 km more because after Port Blanford, the highway veers north-west through the Terra Nova National Park. Fortunately we had taken a lunch with us on the train, for it took nearly three hours to get to Gander, and by the time our car was unloaded it was five o'clock in the afternoon. We decided to have supper there before going on the fifty more miles to Grand Falls, where we planned to spend the night although we had no reservations at any hotel. A few miles outside Gander, on the road to Glenwood, we visited an old friend and former co-worker at the *News*, Billy Temple. He was now retired there with his lovely wife, but still writing a weekly column entitled, "The Old Grouch." We stayed some time there discussing old times, and by the time we reached Norris Arm it was already dark. Driving through that town we got a flat tire and a strange thing happened there. I got out to change the tire and discovered we had no lug wrench. The car was only a year old and this was the first flat we'd had. I remembered passing a service station a few hundred feet back, so I walked back and asked if I could buy a lug wrench there. They had none for sale but would loan me one. I took them up on their offer and after changing the tire drove back with the tool. As I was getting back into the car, a man asked me if I was going on to Grand Falls, and I said I was. He asked, "Have you got reservations?" I replied, "No." Then he said, "In that case I won't ask you for a lift." Then he walked away leaving me just about dumbfounded. My wife and I wondered what the heck did our not-having-reservations in Grand Falls have to do with his not-wanting a lift? We would soon find out. About twenty miles past Norris Arm, as we were driving along the wide unpaved highway in the darkness, we came upon a wooden barrier completely blocking the road. That's very strange, we thought, there must be a detour or something. I got out of the car and walked back the road and saw a narrow road leading down from the highway. No road signs or anything, but we decided to drive down and see where it would bring us. We drove down the hill only a couple of hundred feet and nearly into a big body of water. What a fright! The road ran straight into it. I'll never forget that black water with small wisps of fog rising from the surface. I stopped just in time. Now we were really confused. Carefully turning the car around, we drove back up to the barrier and again got out and looked about in the darkness. Then we saw the headlights of two cars coming towards us, and without any hesitation, the cars both turned down that small side road. We figured they must know something we didn't, so once again we turned and drove down behind them. The two cars were stopped at the water's edge. What we didn't know was that this was the great 400-foot-wide Exploits River, and there was no bridge over it yet. In the distance out of the blackness across the river slowly came a light. As it got closer we could see in the car's headlights this big wooden raft on a bunch of oil drums. There was a steel cable stretching all the way across the river, anchored on both sides, and two pulleys attached to the raft to keep it from being swept down the river. On one side of the raft was a fishing boat attached and this would pull the raft slow-

Train carried autos 80 miles from Clarenville to Gander in 1955, before the Trans-Canada Highway was completed. *Photo by Frank Kennedy*

Makeshift ferry carried cars across 400 foot-wide Exploits River. *Photo by Frank Kennedy*

Dotted line indicates present location of Trans-Canada Highway on the north shore of Birchy lake. Auto is facing east on old road.1500 foot Mount Sykes at left. *Photo by Frank Kennedy*

Encouraging road sign near Gander marked end of 20 miles of burnt-over countryside. *Photo by Frank Kennedy*

The Trans-Canada Highway in 1955. *Photo by Frank Kennedy*

The Trans-Canada Highway in 1995. *Photo by Frank Kennedy*

ly across the river. As the contrivance hit the bank, a man threw down a make-shift ramp, and the two cars drove carefully on to the raft. We did the same. The man came to our car window and asked for the fare. I think it was five dollars. I paid him and he asked, "Is there only three cars?" I said, "I guess so." He muttered something about there's supposed to be four cars and then pulled up the ramp.

When we were nearly across the river, we looked back and saw two cars coming down that side road to the water's edge. We heard later that this "river ferry "stopped operating as darkness fell, but if two or more cars wanted to cross later, they could phone ahead and make reservations with the operator and he would come over at the appointed time. Someone had obviously called ahead and made reservations for four cars at ten o'clock, and two of them were just a little bit late arriving. Lucky for us! Now we knew why that guy didn't want a lift. Rumor at the time had it that the operator was a buddy of Premier Smallwood, who was urged to delay the building of the bridge as long as possible, so that he could continue to make a fortune in the summer, and spend his winters in Florida. I don't know whether the other two cars got over that night, but we drove on to Grand Falls and found a vacancy at Baird's Hotel and spent a good night there. Continuing our journey the next day, we drove west to Badger, then north up the Hall's Bay Line thirty miles to South Brook. This road was very narrow and through deep woods. A large highway sign reminded us to "USE YOUR ASHTRAYS—VERY NARROW ROAD." That road has since been rebuilt and widened and is now part of the T.C.H. On that day there was a hang-up half way along the road, and a long line of cars. I walked up to see what was happening, and there were fruit and vegetables all over the road. A big truck had overturned and we were held up for three hours. It was a nice summer day, so it wasn't so bad.

Going west from Halls Bay we passed along the north shore of Birchy Lake, a nice scenic route; actually, it's better than the present route of the T.C.H., which passes on the south side of the lake. The remainder of our trip was relatively uneventful, and we went only as far as St. George's, to the home of my wife's sister and her husband, Joan and Terry White. We did notice on our return trip that before we came to the Exploits River, there were signs all over the place saying, "FERRY-FERRY-FERRY." Too bad there were none on the other side.

Churchill Falls Power Comes On Stream

"It's high time the Hamilton [Churchill] Falls had a bridle "-
—Winston Churchill.

On July 16, 1972, the most expensive project in the history of Newfoundland, and the largest construction project in Canada to that date, was officially opened by the Prime Minister of Canada, Pierre Elliott Trudeau. It was the Churchill Falls Power and we covered it for CBC TV. Back in 1952, only three years after Confederation, Premier Smallwood went to England to try and raise the $800 million necessary to develop the massive undertaking, and while there, addressed a meeting of the prestigious Federation of British Industries. He said he was there to offer them "the biggest real estate deal of the century" He would give them a piece of land the size of England with all the natural resources thereon. He would give them the timber rights, the mineral rights and the water power rights, if in return they would develop and harness the mighty power that had been wasting away for untold centuries. Smallwood even managed an interview with Prime Minister Winston Churchill and explained his great plan. Churchill was very impressed and encouraged Smallwood to get on with what Churchill called, "The Grand Concept." He already knew of the tremendous waterfall in the wilderness and said, "It's high time the Hamilton Falls had a bridle." (Smallwood changed the name to Churchill Falls in 1965.)

As a direct result of his speech to the federation and his meeting with Churchill, seven United Kingdom banking and industrial firms got together, led by the far-sighted Edmund de Rothschild, and formed a syndicate. It was the British Newfoundland Corporation (BRINCO). This was the company responsible for signing the now infamous sixty-five-year contract. Smallwood took the credit initially for the deal, but as the years wore on, and the sourness of the agreement began to develop, he denied signing it himself. That was true. He himself did not sign the papers, but he was well aware of the arrangement and fully sanctioned it. And it was not just a simple signing. Although BRINCO was incorporated in 1953, thirteen years would elapse before the first sod was turned to mark the start of the immense project in October, 1966. Over the years the arguments between BRINCO and Quebec had been ongoing. BRINCO wanted permission to string power lines across Quebec and sell power to New York. Quebec Premier Johnson said, "No!" Smallwood then declared he would bring the power across the Strait of Belle Isle, down through the island, across the Cabot Strait, on through Nova Scotia and New Brunswick and into the States that way. Quebec told him to go ahead: "We can do without your power. We can develop the mighty James Bay and build nuclear and oil fired plants." The idea of construction work worth hundreds of millions of dollars going on outside their province was also a thorn in the side for Quebec. No agreement could be reached until 1965 when the federal government changed its taxation policy on power produced by private companies. BRINCO at last could meet the demands of Hydro Quebec. Hindsight is 20/20 of course, but at the time it seemed like a fair deal, and by no stretch of the imagination could anyone forsee the drastic rise in inflation and energy costs that would occur over the next thirty years. Anyway, it was basically a "take it or leave it" deal. Smallwood had virtually tried all around the world to have someone come up with the $800 million necessary to develop the Churchill, when his only collateral was a big chunk of wilderness with a big waterfall in the middle. No takers.

It was a big waterfall, no question. At fifty feet higher than the mighty Niagara, when closed off and run through eleven turbines, it would produce enough electricity to light ten million households. Six million horsepower! (That word has nothing to do with the strength of an animal, but is the amount on energy required to lift 15 tons one foot in one minute.) The project was a tremendous boost to the Newfoundland economy, a fact hardly ever mentioned these days, but for over five years thousands found employment there, and in the peak year 1970, more than six thousand people worked on the job. Also, the off-site employment for turbine and generator manufacture required the equivalent of six hundred people working for a six year period. Churchill Falls Newfoundland Limited had been formed as a subsidiary of BRINCO to actually carry out the work. The work force in Labrador was spread over hundreds of square miles. Ninety dams had to be built to hold back the water when the Churchill River was plugged above the falls. 40 miles of dams were eventually put in place, with an average height of thirty feet. The highest is 120 feet and the longest 4 miles. Seven existing lakes were brought together to form one huge body of water. When all this water, aided by thirty inches of rain per year, backed up to the dams, the 2700 square mile Smallwood Reservoir was formed. This lake is now 100 miles long and from 20 to 40 miles wide. All this water is on the Labrador plateau, more than 1400 feet above sea level. When the water drops 1000 feet through the eleven penstocks to produce the enormous power, it runs on through a gigantic surge chamber and back into the Churchill River once more, and is still 400 feet above sea level. This further drop before reaching that level has the potential for development of more power on the Lower Churchill River. The powerhouse has been blasted out of solid rock and lies 1000 feet underground. The machine room where the eleven generators were installed is the largest non-mining rock chamber in the world. 972 feet long and 80 feet wide, for a total floor space of 77,760 square feet. It is much larger then the much touted ice hockey hall in Lillehammer, Norway, which has only 59,600 square feet of space. Mr. Tom Kierans, unsuccessful promoter of the rock arena for the Southside Hills in St. John's is one of the principle engineers responsible for this major project. Final cost was $950 million plus $360 million for Quebec for stringing the wires across their province and building the necessary substations.

The Official Startup

The inauguration took place in the comparatively remote area at the top of the penstocks. Nevertheless, 2000 people turned out for the event. Most came by bus or car, but several helicopters were chartered by C. F. L. Co. to bring in the scores of VIPs and the media people. Progressive Conservative Premier Frank Moores gave great praise to the people who made the project come about, but especially to former Liberal Premier Joey Smallwood. He said, "When many people felt the project would never come about, there was one man who fought hard to keep the spark alive. He succeeded, and the province of Newfoundland today benefits. That man is Joey Smallwood." He thanked Joey sincerely for bringing it about. Smallwood was in London, England, but sent a telegram to Moores, who, "as chosen leader of Newfoundland will take an honored place in the starting of the mighty Churchill Falls development, and on this historic day, I join with you in spirit, side by side with all Newfoundlanders." Prime Minister Trudeau said, "We stand in awe before the Churchill Falls complex, the largest construction project in the history of Canada and the largest underground powerhouse in the world." Premier Bourassa put in a plug for Quebec, saying it was questionable the gigantic project could have been accomplished without the participation of his province. He added most of the equipment used here came from Quebec, as well as many of the skilled workers.

There was a problem with the actual act of inauguration. There were no switches to be turned on and no buttons to be pushed, as the generators were already running and the power was already on. It was decided to unveil a huge time-capsule. This was a twenty-ton boulder into which would be cemented four brass sealed containers with memorabilia of the day, including agreements, letters of intent, power contracts, etc. The curtain was pulled open by two twelve-year-old children; Girl Guide Debbie Davis, and Boy Scout David Swiggan. A tremendous round of applause echoed through the wilderness. Trudeau then declared the project officially on stream and a very impressive display of fireworks rounded out the program. After the ceremony the two thousand people left the site. The media people were taken by some of the helicopters directly to the airport to catch a 737 jet to Gander and St. John's. This would be the last plane back to St. John's in about a week and we wanted to be on board. We had been in Churchill Falls for two days and while the ceremony was in progress, our personal luggage was transferred from our hotel to the aircraft, compliments of C. F. L. Co. Cameraman Ralph Pottle of CJON and myself had a lot of equipment to pack up at the site and were the last to leave. However, when we got to the two remaining choppers they were both full. Apparently some of the earlier whirlybirds had left with empty seats. One of the pilots assured us he would come back. The plane wouldn't be leaving for over an hour, so there was plenty of time. The two choppers took off and disappeared over the western horizon. We looked around. Here we were alone in the wilderness with not a living soul in sight. Ralph and I sat on our equipment cases and waited. And waited. And waited. One of us would spot something miles away flying over the tundra. "Look!" we would shout. Then, "No. It's only a bird." Finally, with only thirty minutes left for departure time, a small helicopter came and took us on board. It would take a half hour to get to the airport, the pilot told us, so he got on the radio and told the control tower we were on our way, and asked them to hold the plane. The tower said this would not be possible as the jet had to make connections at Gander. We prayed we would make it, especially knowing our personal luggage was on board that aircraft. After thirty minutes we arrived at the airport. The plane was still on the ground, and as our pilot set us down fifty feet away, they were just closing the door of the jet. When they saw us they opened the door again. I told Ralph to run to the terminal building and get our boarding passes while I ran back and forth to the plane with our equipment. We barely made it and had no further problems. Ralph Pottle is now with the CBC.

BEFORE: As we flew over the Churchill Falls before the water was diverted the roar of the water could be heard above the sound of the airplane engines. *Photo by Frank Kennedy*

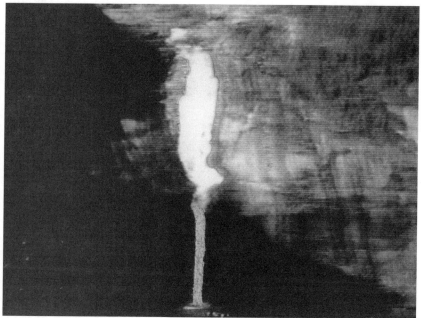

AFTER: Now most of the water goes through eleven huge penstocks leaving the falls almost non-existent. *Photo Courtesy CBC-TV*

Giant six hundred and fifty ton rotor is about to be placed into position in the machine hall at the Churchill Falls power plant. Eleven of these are in operation 1000 feet underground. *Photo Courtesy CBC-TV*

Biggest single source of power in the world, this huge underground machine room is larger than the hockey arena in Lillehammer, Norway. *Illustration by C.F.L Co.*

Seven major hydraulic structures like this regulate flow of water at the Churchill Falls development. When fully opened, each has a capacity of 100,000 cubic feet per second. *Photo by CFL.Co*

Frank Kennedy and Mike Fitzpatrick of CBC take off for the site of Churchill Falls inauguration in 1972.

Odds and Ends

Doug Pike

Some years ago when the phosphorus plant was in operation at Long Harbour the fallout from the smokestack was reported to be causing deformities in some of the wildlife in the area. Doug Pike said it was discovered that all the rabbits there had hare lips.

Aubrey Macdonald

Aubrey told us that when he was a boy, only the very poor would eat or admit to eating lobsters. The shellfish were considered scavengers and hardly fit for human food. Years later the eating of lobsters almost became a status symbol. Aubrey said if he was going to work in the morning and saw lobster shells on his neighbors' garbage can, he would take them off and put them on his garbage can. Aubrey was fired several times by Mr. Bill Galgay, "the chief", but always hired back the next day. On one occasion Aubrey was working in the control room of CBC radio on November 11, when the service from the war memorial was being broadcast live. Mac was not paying much attention to the proceedings being described by Bill Galgay. Suddenly he became aware of the fact that no sound was coming through. "Dead air" is an absolute no-no on radio and figuring Galgay's microphone had become disconnected, quick-thinking Aubrey immediately put on some recorded music. It so happened that at that time the gathering was observing two minutes silence. Out, Aubrey!

Ann Budgell

Some years ago when Jim Morgan was minister of highways, he announced that they would not be plowing the road from Labrador City to Churchill Falls that winter. He said this was for safety reasons, as if people thought the 200 km road was open they might set out by car and be lost in the snowdrifts. Ann Budgell was sent to Confederation Building to question him about this for "Here and Now" and I was there to film the interview. Ann was convinced that the real reason for the step was to save money, but Morgan wouldn't admit that. When the interview was finished and I was taking down my floodlights, Ann said to the minister, "You know, Mr. Morgan, I just got back from Labrador and the people up there think you're full of shit!" His only reply was, "Well, I suppose they're entitled to their own opinion." Ann Budgell tells it like it is. Great reporter!

Doug Peet

Kevin Hanlon, Doug Peet and I were discussing a friend whose wife had just died. Kevin said it must be hard to lose your wife. Doug Peet responded, "It is. I've been trying for years to lose mine." On another occasion, the CBC were tendering me a farewell party upon my retirement after forty-two years of picture taking. Emcee Paul Harrington told how when still in high school, Frank Kennedy bought his first camera, a Baby Brownie, for $1. 20. Paul said at that time Frank hoped that some day he would become a professional photographer. Doug Peet spoke up in a loud voice, "I hope he makes it!"

Rab Carnell

We were shooting an interview with a farmer in a barn for "Land and Sea." I told Rab I'd like to set up the camera in a certain spot, but there was a lot of cow dung where I wanted to put the tripod. Rab grabbed a shovel and started clearing a spot for me, at the same time muttering, "After all these years, I never thought I'd end up shoveling shit for the CBC."

Max Mercer

Max was a freelance cameraman who did a lot of work for the CBC. Unfortunately he developed diabetes and began going blind. Before losing his sight completely, he trained a friend of his to take over the work. One day the Gulf ferry workers went on strike and Max and his assistant were at Port-aux-Basques, shooting the long lineup of cars and trucks. Max was standing on the side of the road just up from the pier and told his friend to go down and get some shots near the ferry. Max would wait there. Max told me that as he stood there with his white cane in hand, some kind gentleman offered to guide him across the street. Max replied, "No thank you, I'm here directing a movie." There was complete silence after that, and Max said he was really sorry he could not see the expression on that good Samaritan's face.

Don Jamieson

One day the late Bren Walsh and I were coming from the Burin Peninsula and Bren wanted to drop in and see his old friend, Don Jamieson at Swift Current. While there Don, who was quite a big man, told this story to Bren:

Back in the early sixties when I was a reporter for the Sunday Herald, we were covering a big game at St. Pat's baseball field. Frank Kennedy was there for the Daily News and was even slimmer than he is today. Kennedy made some remark about food, and I said to him, "Go 'way Kennedy, you look like a refugee from a famine!" With no hesitation, Frank shot back, "Yes, and you look like you caused it!"

Blue Ribbon Entry

When the Summer Games were held in St. John's some years ago the opening ceremonies were spectacular, and the closing ceremonies were touted to be even better and tickets for that event were sold out weeks in advance. I covered some of the regular events for the CBC and had a press pass which consisted of a three-inch badge with a foot-long blue ribbon attached. Although not assigned to the closing ceremonies, I did want to see them and would use my pass to get in. My daughter Florence dearly wanted to be there too, but no tickets were available. It occurred to me that she had entered our cat, "Pritz" in a recent pet show and that animal won first prize as the cat with the most unusual name. The prize was a three-inch badge with a blue ribbon attached. At the closing ceremonies, my daughter wore my press pass, I wore the cat award and we passed through the gate with no questions asked.

Smallwood's Obituary

Joey Smallwood allowed us to take pictures of him for his obituary, knowing they would not be shown until after his death. We filmed him at his Roache's Line home, getting in his car, and driving away from the house. I had asked him to stop before he left the ranch, so that I could go outside and get him exiting the gateway. I said we also wanted a shot of his arrival at his private office on Portugal Cove Road in St. John's, but knowing his record for fast driving, I suggested he go on to town and when we got there he could come out and stage the arrival. That is what happened and Smallwood was very cooperative and so the pictures were used only after he had passed away. The story is told of Joey speeding out the T. C. H. and being chased by a Mountie with red lights flashing. Joey pulled over and when the Mountie walked up to the car, Joey put down his tinted glass window and the surprised policeman exclaimed, "My God!" Joey replied, "Yes, and don't you forget it!"

Final Assignment for the CBC

One of my last assignments with the CBC was one I enjoyed over a number of years. That was filming the annual Christmas message of Lieutenant Governor Anthony Paddon. When I retired in January 1986, I was indeed honored to receive this letter.

GOVERNMENT HOUSE,
ST. JOHN'S,
NEWFOUNDLAND.

January 24th. 1986.

Mr. Frank Kennedy,
23 Newtown Road,
St. John's,
Newfoundland.　A1C 4C9

Dear Mr. Kennedy,

On the eve of your retirement I should like to offer my warmest congratulations for 42 years of service to Newfoundland and elsewhere as a photographer of news, events, documentaries and much else. The quality of your work spoke for itself. I suspect, too, that you will be remembered for your courtesy to your subjects. Most of us have some hesitation about being photographed for public exhibition, but I for one felt very much at ease working with you. I am sure your ability to reassure people and your courtesy must have affected your work favourably.

You can retire in the certainty of having done a first rate job, both in artistry and accuracy. Countless thousands of us have seen and enjoyed your work, and would wish you well throughout a long and contented retirement.

Sincerely,

W. Anthony Paddon

Lieutenant-Governor.

Frank J. Kennedy

The Harvey Road Fire, 1992—Worst Fire in St. John's in 100 Years

Although retired when this conflagration took place on December 21, 1992, I did as usual take pictures, but was so appalled at how this fire spread from such a small beginning, that I just had to write my eye-witness account of the fire that did $3. 5 million damage. In terms of property destruction, it was the worst fire in the city in 100 years. The fire started in the Church Lad's Brigade (CLB) Armory and spread to the Social Services building next door, then across Harvey Road, and destroyed an entire block, including eleven businesses and a dozen homes. The Dominion supermarket, next door west, was also burned to the ground. One hundred people were left entirely homeless, and at the height of the blaze, five hundred people were ordered out of various houses in the area. I've seen a lot of fires in my forty-two years on the job, and always had the greatest admiration for the firefighters, but never did I see one that got away from them as this one did. I can't understand it. Nevertheless, the acting fire marshal at the time did an investigation and recommended no public inquiry be held. Very strange. He said the probable cause of the fire was an electrical malfunction in the female washroom area.

On that night, just four days before Christmas, my wife and I were driving around, admiring the Christmas lights, and were on our way home shortly after eight o'clock. Going east on LeMarchant Road near McKinlay Motors, I heard a siren behind and pulled over to let a fire truck pass. I remarked that it was the yellow truck from the West End station, unusual for it to be coming this far east. When we reached the bus terminal, we noticed the truck was stopped near the top of Long's Hill. Then we saw a small amount of smoke coming from the alleyway between the CLB Armory and the Dominion. I intended driving by, but a fireman directed me down Long's Hill. I pulled in and parked near the top of the hill; we were now opposite the CLB and could see some smoke still coming from between the two buildings. My wife suggested the smoke was probably coming from a dumpster that we knew was located on the supermarket parking lot. I said, "No, that's definitely wood burning. I can smell it. I'll walk back and take a look." I did that and for the first time saw small flames, only about a foot long, coming from three places in the wall of the CLB, a few feet from each other, near the ground. It was pitch dark in the alleyway and firemen were using flashlights. I went back to the car and told my wife I would stick around for a while. She asked me to drive her home first, which I did, and went into our house on Newtown Road and changed my overcoat for a heavier parka. It was a very frosty night. As I was leaving the house, my wife asked, "Aren't you going to take your camera?" I answered, "No. I don't think there's going to be much to this." Famous last words!

I drove down Newtown Road, down Parade Street and on to the police parking lot which was almost vacant, and parked just above the supermarket parking lot. Just as I expected, there was no fire at all to be seen, not a spark! Still some smoke, about the same as when we had left ten minutes earlier. After another five minutes, the smoke seemed to die down, so I figured the blaze was under control and I might as well go home. Before doing so, I decided to go over and look at the east side of the Armory. I drove across the parking lot to where I had a clear view of that side of the building. What I saw changed my mind about the fire being under control. A small amount of black smoke was coming from under the eaves and I thought, "Oh, Oh. It's not out yet!" The fire department ladder truck was parked on the super-market parking lot, with the big ladder resting on the low roof of the CLB extension. A fireman was on this roof trying to get a chain saw started. He finally did after several tries, and disappeared from view towards the front of the building. Another man on the ground was chopping at a wooden shutter by the light of a flashlight. When he removed the shutter, there was no fire to be seen. Just darkness and more smoke. After another four or five minutes a flame suddenly burst up through the lower roof and leapt ten or twelve feet into the air, and a minute later flames burst out through one of the upper windows. I thought, "Oh no! After all this time it's getting away from them" I began to realize I should have taken my camera and drove home to get it.

CLB Armory is engulfed in flames as conflagration burns out of control.
Photo by Frank Kennedy

Flames break through the rear of the Church Lads Brigade Armory on
December 21, 1992. *Photo by Frank Kennedy*

When I got back to the scene, police had barred off the top of Parade Street to traffic, so I walked down to the police parking lot. Flames were now coming from all sides of the CLB building. I took some pictures. I was startled by the sound of exploding small arms ammunition, as if hundreds of fire crackers were going off in there. When the roof collapsed, I went down to have a look at the front of the building. As I walked past the Dominion supermarket, the sprinkler system alarm bell was ringing loudly, although there was no sign of fire yet as I looked through the large plate glass windows. Hundreds of people had already gathered, but there were no police lines up as yet. By now the fire was completely out of control. The heat on Harvey Road was tremendous. The wind was blowing the flames across the street. I saw a power pole catch fire and the wires actually burn off with lightning-like flashes, and drop to the ground. A Light and Power truck was parked nearby, but the men couldn't get close enough to cut the wires, so they called the sub-station and had the power in the area shut off. Fire trucks parked in front of the building began backing off from the searing heat, which soon ignited the houses on the other side of Harvey Road. It was now impossible for firemen or anyone else to even be on that section of Harvey Road. I found myself standing near the top of Long's Hill, taking pictures of the inferno. Flames were gushing from windows of the CLB like giant blow-torches. A policeman approached and told me to move back. I was tempted from force of habit to say, "CBC!" But I said nothing, just stood there with my little camera and clicked another shot. Then the policeman came at me, gesturing and shouting, "Get Back!" The realization finally sunk in. I had no special status anymore. No press pass. No permission to cross police lines. No big press camera. No great rapport with the police and firemen anymore. No nothing. I moved back and melted into the crowd. Just one more spectator among the thousands at a big fire in St. John's. But it had certainly been a wonderful career.

30

Church Lads Brigade Armory on Harvey Road before the fire. *Photo by Frank Kennedy*

CLB Armory on December 21, 1992. *Photo by Frank Kennedy*

A Few Extra Shots

A city fireman, with breathing apparatus, checks a cat he has just rescued from a house fire on Hamilton Street in St. John s in the early sixties. The cat was okay. Daily News *Photo by Frank Kennedy*

The old three story infirmary was commonly known as, "The Poor House," and was located on Sudbury Street just off Water Street. It was a wooden building and patients with mental disabilities were locked up on the third floor. In 1965 all residents were moved to the new Hoyles Home and the old building was torn down.

The Hoyles Home on Portugal Cove Road was officially opened by Premier Smallwood on November 3, 1965. It is named in honour of the first native born premier of Newfoundland, Sir Hugh Hoyles, who served as premier and attorney general from 1861 to 1865.
Photos by Frank Kennedy

Prince Charles observes Lady Diana as she speaks with Premier Brian Peckford during their visit to North America's most easterly point on June 24, 1983. A government official addresses the gathering.

During a "walk about," Lady Diana is filmed by CBC cameraman Frank Kennedy, right, as she speaks with an admirer.

Back in 1958, this truck was being loaded with steel beams which were too long for the truck. As the loading continued, the rear of the truck swung down to the ground and the front came up. As I was about to snap a picture, Ed Doran walked into the scene and presented this "strong man" pose. The *Daily News* printed the photo.

Anyone who knows trout will immediately recognize this as a real mud trout. We dreamed up this one for a special May 24 issue of the *News*. It's a combination of three photos. The fish was all of eight inches long. *Photos by Frank Kennedy*

Bruce Neal could have easily joined the circus with this startling demonstration back in the sixties. He tried to teach us how to do this, but when he said, "You have to get a match ready and then take a mouthful of kerosene oil," we said, "Stop right there!" He is a successful business man, now retired.

Three CBC staffers check an award-winning commercial they produced for the "Poppe Shop" in 1976. The late Chris Franzen, wrote the ad, Kennedy filmed it and John St. George did the editing. The commercial was adjudged by the TV Board of Canada as being one of the top ten produced in Canada that year.

Cameraman Kennedy and the late Ted Withers cover an annual regatta at Quidi Vidi in the late sixties.

Rafe O'Neill doesn't seem worried about this pre-historic monster stepping into his boat at Big Country Pond. He was amused, though, when he saw this picture.

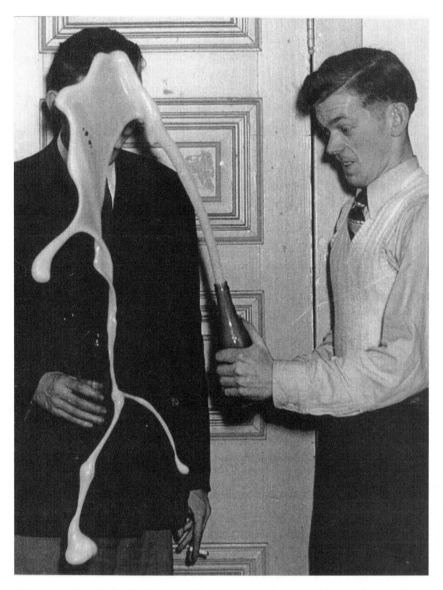

Photographer Nels Squires makes some pretty potent home brew. One day at the "*News*" he opened a bottle and it nearly hit the ceiling. I got my camera and asked him to open another and this was the result. For photo buffs, the exposure was 1/1000 sec with F.P. flashbulb.

When the Cathedral in St. John's was raised to the status of Minor
Basilica in 1955, a huge scaffold was built six feet below the ceiling, so
that it could be painted and interlaced with genuine gold leaf. Here,
Frank Kennedy checks out the light with his meter.

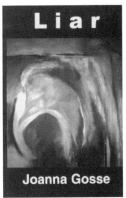